PRAISE FOR TIM WISE

"Tim Wise is one of the most brilliant, articulate and courageous critics of white privilege in the nation. His considerable rhetorical skills, his fluid literary gifts and his relentless search for the truth make him a critical ally in the fight against racism and a true soldier in the war for social justice. His writing and thinking constitute a bulwark of common sense, and uncommon wisdom, on the subject of race, politics and culture. He is a national treasure."

—**Michael Eric Dyson**, University Professor, Georgetown University, and best-selling author of more than a dozen books on race.

"Tim Wise is one of those rare 'public intellectuals' that numerous authors have suggested are becoming extinct in this society. He is evidence that this is not the case . . . in my judgment, he is the very best of the white anti-racism writers and commentators working in the U.S. media today. . . ."

—**Joe Feagin**, Graduate Research Professor of Sociology, Texas A&M, and author of more than twenty books on race issues.

"(Wise's) work is revolutionary, and those who react negatively are simply afraid of hearing the truth. . . ."
—**Robin D.G. Kelley**, Professor of History, University of Southern California, author of *Race Rebels,* and *Yo' Mama's Disfunktional!*

"One of the brilliant voices of our time."
—**Molefi Kete Asante**, Professor of African American Studies, Temple University, creator of the first doctoral program in African American Studies in the United States.

"Wise is the nation's leading antiracist author/activist. . . ."
—**David Naguib Pellow**, professor of Ethnic Studies, University of Minnesota.

"(His) is the clearest thinking on race I've seen in a long while written by a white writer . . . right up there with the likes of historians Howard Zinn and Herb Aptheker as far as I'm concerned."
—**Dr. Joyce King**, Associate Provost, Medgar Evers College, Brooklyn, NY.

BETWEEN BARACK
AND A HARD PLACE

Racism and White Denial
in the Age of Obama

Tim Wise

CITY LIGHTS BOOKS / OPEN MEDIA SERIES
San Francisco

The Open Media Series is edited by Greg Ruggiero and archived by
the Tamiment Library, New York University.

Cover design: Pollen

Library of Congress Cataloging-in-Publication Data

Wise, Tim J.
 Between Barack and a hard place : racism and white denial in the age
of Obama / by Tim Wise.
     p. cm.
 Includes bibliographical references.
 ISBN 978-0-87286-500-6
1. Whites—Race identity—United States. 2. Whites—United States—
Attitudes. 3. Racism—United States. 4. United States—Race relations.
5. Obama, Barack. I. Title.

 E184.A1.W57 2009
 305.800973—dc22

                    2008048296

City Lights Books are published at the City Lights Bookstore,
261 Columbus Avenue, San Francisco, CA 94133.

www.citylights.com

Contents

Preface

On November 4, 2008, at a little after 10:00 p.m. Eastern Standard Time, television networks began announcing the big news: Senator Barack Obama had been elected 44th president of the United States, thereby becoming the first person of color to win the office in the nation's history. Immediately, discussion turned to the historicity of the moment, and with good reason. For a nation built on a foundation of slavery, disenfranchisement, and white domination, the election of a man of color (and a man who, according to the racial taxonomy that has long existed in the United States, is indeed black) to the highest office in the land, is of no small import.

Millions of new voters, especially voters of color, had turned out in record numbers to cast their ballots for Barack Obama. In the days that followed, African American men and women who thought this moment might never happen, spoke of the pride they felt, having come so far in the past four decades, from a time when merely registering black people to vote could and did result in death. That Obama's victory says something about the United States, and about race and racism in this nation, is hard to deny.

But what it says, and what it doesn't say, is ultimately

not determined by the feelings of voters, however joyful they may be about Obama's victory. What Obama's political rise says about racism in America is to be determined by an honest appraisal of the real conditions on the ground in this place, not for Barack Obama, but for approximately 90 million persons of color in all: black, Latino, Asian American and Pacific Islander, indigenous persons, and Middle Easterners. When that appraisal is conducted, the racial and ethnic reality of the United States is sure to be seen as far more complex than some might like to think. For while the individual success of persons of color, as with Obama, is meaningful (and at this level was unthinkable merely a generation ago), the larger systemic and institutional realities of life in America suggest the ongoing salience of a deep-seated cultural malady—racism—which has been neither eradicated nor even substantially diminished by Obama's victory.

Herein I will explore what the political ascent of Barack Obama might mean, and more importantly what it doesn't mean, about race, about the power of whiteness in early twenty-first-century America, and about America itself. This I will do in the form of two essays, the first of which argues that contrary to the beliefs of many, the evidence is clear: systemic racial discrimination and profound inequity of opportunity continue to mark the lives of persons of color, Obama's own successes notwithstanding. Furthermore, not only does the success of Barack

Obama not signify the death of white racism as a personal or institutional phenomenon, if anything, it may well signal the emergence of an altogether new kind of racism. Consider this, for lack of a better term, Racism 2.0, or enlightened exceptionalism, a form that allows for and even celebrates the achievements of individual persons of color, but only because those individuals generally are seen as different from a less appealing, even pathological black or brown rule. If whites come to like, respect, and even vote for persons of color like Barack Obama, but only because they view them as having "transcended" their blackness in some way, to claim that the success of such candidates proves the demise of racism makes no sense at all. If anything, success on these terms confirms the salience of race and the machinations of white hegemony. That 43 percent of whites voted for Obama—more than voted for any white Democratic candidate since Lyndon Johnson in 1964—is impressive, to be sure, but perhaps less so than many would like to think.

In short, the 2008 presidential election may not have been a contest in which racism was vying against antiracism, so much as one in which two different types of racism were competing for predominance. On the one hand was old-fashioned bigotry, or Racism 1.0, which could have caused enough whites to vote against Obama for racial reasons as to have ensured his defeat. This is the kind of bigotry that has long marked the nation's history:

the kind that, in its most extreme moments has precipitated racist murder, lynching, and terror on a grand scale; the kind that led to dozens of white-on-black riots in city after city for much of the early 1900s; the kind that precipitated restrictive covenants and "neighborhood improvement associations" to block persons of color from moving into white neighborhoods; the kind that even now animates hate groups and hate crimes when taken to its illogical conclusion. It is racism with which we are, as a nation, familiar, even if we remain sadly naïve as to the depths of its depravity. And that familiarity allows us to know it when we see it, as we occasionally did in the run-up to the election, in hostile and unhinged e-mails attacking Obama for racial or religious reasons, or in Internet videos showing blatantly racist supporters of Obama's opponent, Senator John McCain, engaged in only the most thinly veiled racist invective. On the other hand, however, was Racism 2.0—a far less easily recognized type—which could allow him to win the presidency, but only because of his ability to ease white fears and transcend his still-problematic blackness, biracial though it may be. While Racism 1.0 appears to have suffered a defeat this time out—and for that, we can all be grateful—let us not overlook the possibility that Racism 2.0 may have been in full effect, and ultimately the reason for Obama's victory. And if that is true—a subject we will explore shortly—then there remains a great amount of work to be done.

Likewise, if Obama's win has the effect of creating a new archetype or model of acceptable blackness—in other words, if whites come to "need" black folks to be Obama-like in style, affect, erudition, and educational background in order to be considered competent or trustworthy—his singular victory could actually create higher barriers for the bulk of African Americans. Whereas whites have long been able to run the gamut of observable intelligence, articulateness, accent, and erudition and still become president, or obtain other high-ranking positions in the private sector, for instance, people of color have long worried about being tokenized, and accepted only when they make whites sufficiently comfortable or don't seem "too black" in the way many whites still perceive the larger black community. If Obama's success reinforces that tendency to isolate acceptable blacks from those who are "unacceptable," the consequences for overall racial equity could be negative, rather than positive.

In the second essay, I explore the unique challenge to white America posed by Obama's candidacy and pending presidency. While overt racists will counsel backlash, and use Obama's rise to suggest that America is descending into a pit of cultural decay, and while mainstream commentators will counsel celebration, and use Obama as proof positive that racism is no longer a potent social force with which we must grapple, there is another option, at once more level-headed and yet aspirational, to which we might turn. That option is to seize the moment, to channel the energy unleashed by the Obama campaign, to focus those who have believed so much in him and his mantra of "change" into productive antiracism and social justice work. The choice is to use this opening to develop and strengthen white antiracist identity, to insist on the audacity of truth and not just hope, to demand better of ourselves than perhaps even we thought possible. Just as Obama has issued a challenge to black folks to be more responsible for the problems in their communities—in part a message he sincerely believes, of course, but also one intended to make whites more comfortable with his candidacy—so too must whites take personal responsibility for ongoing racism, racial injustice, and the unearned privileges we continue to reap as a result. In other words, while it is certainly advisable for persons of color to take responsibility for their lives, no matter the presence of racism, it is just as important for whites to take responsibility for our mess, including the mess of racism and privilege, irrespective of how we believe (often incorrectly) black and brown folks are behaving. Personal responsibility is a two-way street, in other words.

It is this call for "200 percent responsibility" that I hope will resonate with those inspired thus far by Obama, and move them from a focus on his personal success to a more liberating and collective vision of progress. In other words, the challenge to the nation—and for my money, especially for white folks—is to channel the energy and the inspiration of concepts like "hope" and "change" into constructive, meaningful endeavors for real social justice. The whole history of the struggle for freedom and true democracy suggests we will have to hold Obama accountable, as would be true with any president, and never become complacent, convinced that he has either the desire or ability to do the work for us. We must remember, it was never about Obama, and it isn't now.

I should say here a few words about terminology used in this book, seeing as how misunderstanding is common when race is the subject being discussed. When I use the term "race" or refer to persons as "black," "white," or "persons of color," I am not suggesting that these are concepts with even the slightest degree of scientific meaning. Indeed, most scientists now reject the notion of race as a biological or genetic construct. Rather, I use the terms in their social sense. Race has meaning not because there are "white genes," or "Asian genes," or "black blood" or "Latino blood," but because it has been given meaning in the laws and customs of a society. Just as the women killed in Salem, Massachusetts, in 1692 weren't really witches, and yet the belief that they were ensured their oppression and death, so too can race have meaning due to social circumstance, even if those being oppressed by the concept are not truly biologically different, in any meaningful way, from those doing the oppressing. To be white is to be a person, typically, of European descent and capable of being viewed as a member of the dominant racial group in the United States. To be black is to be, typically, a person of African descent, dark enough to be considered a member of that group that was historically at or near the bottom (along with indigenous persons) of the nation's racial hierarchy. To be a person of color is simply to be anything other than white, in the eyes of most Americans. These categories are fluid, to be sure, and often contested, but in social terms they remain quite real, such that they describe, with frightening precision, the likely social status of most persons caught in their categories.

In the case of Barack Obama, of course, as many have noted, he is a man of biracial ancestry: the son of a white mother from Kansas and a black father from Kenya. While it is valid and valuable to note Obama's biraciality—especially given the growing number of biracial persons in the United States whose racial identity is often ignored, or who feel as though they are forced to "choose sides" in claiming an identity for themselves—it is also worth pointing out that throughout U.S. history and still today, to be biracial hardly erases one salient fact: a person so designated will typically be seen as a member of whichever group is lowest in the racial hierarchy. So, to be black and white in terms of parentage is to be black. To be white and Asian is to be seen and likely treated as Asian, and so on. This is not to deny the unique forms of discrimination to which biracial people may occasionally be subjected *as* biracial persons, but it is to note that the racism directed their way is most often aimed at the darkest and least white aspect of their heritage. And so, while ancestrally biracial, in the social sense, as a resident of the United States, Barack Obama is incontestably black.

The term racism, as I use it, can and does mean two things: first, an ideological belief in the racial or cultural superiority or inferiority of certain people defined racially as members of a group; and secondly, as a system of inequity based on race, or perceived racial difference. In other words, it is both an idea and a structure of institutions, in which policies, practices, and procedures produce inequitable outcomes. As with other "isms" (capitalism, communism, socialism, fascism, etc.), so too racism is more than merely an ideology. In the United States, racism has taken on particular historical forms, such as enslavement, genocidal land grabs, segregation, and racialized violence; and it has in practice amounted to one specific kind of racism: namely, white supremacy. And so when I use the term white supremacy, I do not mean neo-Nazism or Klan activity. Rather, I mean the entire structure of American institutions, historically and still too often today.

I wish to thank Greg Ruggiero at City Lights for suggesting I write this book, Elaine Katzenberger for agreeing to publish it, and my wife Kristy and our children, Ashton and Rachel, for putting up with me while I got it done.

Even more, I thank my family for their love and devotion, their support and counsel, and the joy they have brought into my life. I also wish to thank those persons who have supported my work throughout the years—you know who you are—and who always manage to give me helpful feedback when I most need it. May you continue to believe in me, and may I continue to deserve whatever respect I have managed to earn so far.

Tim Wise
Nashville, Tennessee
December 2008

ONE

Barack Obama, White Denial and the Reality of Racism

Once Barack Obama became the Democratic Party's nominee for president of the United States, two questions emerged most prominently in media and personal discussions of his candidacy. The first of these, most often put forward by those who were seeking to draw rather sweeping and positive conclusions from their query, was typically posed as, "What does it say about race in America that a black man now stands on the precipice of becoming, arguably, the most powerful person in the world?" The second, presented somewhat more skeptically than the first, and more likely offered up by those whose hopefulness was a bit more tempered by an appreciation of history, most often sounded like this: "Is white America really ready for a black president?"

While we can hardly be surprised at how quickly these became the principal questions asked in the run-up to the November 2008 election, both nonetheless stemmed from premises that were largely false, or at least glaringly problematic. And as with any question that emanates from a false or incomplete starting point, such interrogations as these ultimately led down mundane analytic corridors, to destinations that, although interesting, were never truly the places to which we needed to travel.

For while the political ascent of Barack Obama, culminating with his victory in November over challenger John McCain, certainly says something about race, what it says is far from that which most—including those typically asking the question in the first place—seem to believe. Yes, it suggests that blind and irrational bigotry of the kind that animated so much white opinion for so long in the United States may well have receded (though not as much as we'd like to think, a subject to which I'll return below). But given the evidence regarding entrenched racial inequities in employment, education, health care, criminal justice, housing and elsewhere—and the studies indicating these are due in large measure to discrimination, either past, present, or a combination of the two—it most definitely does not suggest that racism has been truncated as an ongoing social problem for persons of color generally.

Though Obama's victory falls well short of proving that racism has been vanquished in America, for reasons I will explore shortly, it is still worth noting some of the positive aspects of the Obama victory when it comes to race. For although I will insist that his rise says far less than many would suggest, we would do well to at least note a few of the beneficial outcomes, so we know what we have to build on in the future.

First, Obama's election to the presidency demonstrates that old-fashioned racism (or what I call in this volume Racism 1.0), though still far too prevalent in the nation, is capable of being defeated, especially when an effective coalition is put together, and when those who otherwise might fall back into patterns of bias and discrimination can be convinced that their interests (economic, for instance) should outweigh their tendency to act on the basis of skin color. Given the harrowing state of the American economy as voters went to the polls in November, and given the Obama campaign's message that his opponent would only provide tax relief to the wealthiest Americans while largely continuing the economic policies of the Bush administration, many voters (including white working-class voters who had been turning against Democrats for a generation) turned to Obama. Even if they harbored ongoing prejudices toward African Americans generally (and evidence suggests that many still did), they were prepared to vote their pocketbooks and break with a long tradition, stretching back decades, whereby so many of them had ignored economic interests for the sake of apparent "racial bonding," against communities of color.

Especially heartening was the fact that part of the strategy for gaining the support of white working-class voters was to directly confront them on their racism when it was expressed, rather than finessing it. Labor leader Richard Trumka, for instance, as well as other labor organizers and Obama's own campaign in Ohio developed strategies for taking on white racism directly, rather than trying to sidestep it, in the hopes that voters would simply do the right thing for economic reasons alone. By calling out white racism and forcing white working folks to think about the irrationality of racial bonding—especially in the face of an economic free fall—these organizers planted the seeds of potential cross-racial alliance, which, if tended carefully, could bear fruit in the future.[1]

Secondly, and on a related note, the level of cross-racial collaboration (especially among youth) that made Obama's victory possible was something rarely seen in American politics, or history. Although many, including myself, would rather see such mobilizing take place in arenas other than mainstream electoral politics, the fact is, efforts of this nature have to start somewhere. For young people who forged real and meaningful movement relationships in the Obama campaign, the possibility that they may continue to engage in grassroots organizing in years to come—and much of it around issues of racial justice—cannot be ignored. Long-term sustained activism is always more likely for those who have formed those genuine relationships and worked together for a common purpose, as so many young blacks, whites, Latinos and Asian Americans did in this election cycle. Likewise, that so many of the Obama campaigners witnessed racism up close and personal—while either canvassing or making phone calls for the campaign—can only have served to heighten these folks' sensitivity to the problem of racism in America. So although the average white person may view Obama's win as evidence of the death of racism (more on this below), those who worked on his behalf will have a hard time coming to that conclusion, having seen and heard so much raw and unexpurgated bigotry on the campaign trail.[2]

Finally, Obama's win indicates that when a person of color has the opportunity to make his case day after day, for at least a year and a half (and really more, since Obama had been introduced to the public four years earlier during the 2004 Democratic National Convention), he is fully capable of demonstrating to the satisfaction of millions of whites (if still not most), his intelligence, wisdom, and leadership capabilities, sufficiently to win the job for which he is in effect, interviewing. So far so good.

But the bad news, and let us not forget it, is that most job interviews don't last for eighteen months, and don't involve millions of decision-makers, where at least in theory the biases of some can be canceled out by the open-mindedness of others. Rather, most job-seekers are facing a mere handful of evaluators, often only one, and if there is any significant bias in the heart or mind of that person (or if that person adheres, even subconsciously, to negative stereotypes about folks of color), the job applicant who is black or brown faces an uphill climb that Obama's success cannot erase or transform. Likewise, most persons of color don't have the luxury of whipping out their memoir when applying for a mortgage loan, while searching for an apartment, or when they are stopped by a police officer on suspicion of illegal activity and saying, "Here, read this; it'll show you what a great guy I am." Most folks of color face far less deliberative snap judgments on the part of employers, landlords, teachers, and cops, and in those instances, the ability of racial bias to taint the process of evaluation is of no small concern.

So, rather than ask what Obama's success means in terms of race and racism in the United States in the twenty-first century, the better question may be what doesn't his success mean for those things? What does it *not* tell us about how far we've come, and how far we still have to go?

As for the second of the two most often asked questions, while many whites may well not have been prepared to vote for a black—or as some may prefer, biracial—man for the presidency, there is another issue almost completely overlooked by the press: the possibility that Obama might well have won the nation's highest office in spite of ongoing traditional white racism, and yet because of a newer, slicker Racism 2.0, in which whites hold the larger black community in low regard and adhere, for instance, to any number of racist stereotypes about African Americans— and yet carve out acceptable space for individuals such as Obama who strike them as different, as exceptions who are not like the rest. That this "enlightened exceptionalism" manages to accommodate individual people of color, even as it continues to look down upon the larger mass of black and brown America with suspicion, fear, and contempt, suggests the fluid and shape-shifting nature of racism. It indicates that far from vanishing, racism has become more sophisticated and that Obama's rise could, at least in part, stem from the triumph of racism, albeit of a more seemingly ecumenical type than that to which we have grown accustomed.

If some whites are willing to vote for a person of color, but only to the extent they are able to view that person as racially unthreatening, as different from "regular" black people, as somehow less than truly black, or as having "transcended race" (a term used with regularity to describe Obama over the past few years), then white racism remains quite real, quite powerful, and quite operative in the life of the nation. More than that, even in the case of the electoral success of a man of color, it might well have remained central to the outcome. The only question, really, was which kind of racism was likely to show up most prominently on election day? Would it be the traditional old-fashioned kind, rooted in conscious bigotry and hate, the Racism 1.0, which historically has caused many whites to act toward black folks with suspicion, violence, distrust, fear, and anxiety, and which—if it is prevalent enough— could have resulted in Obama's defeat? Or would it be the newer, slicker, enlightened exceptionalism, or Racism 2.0, which still holds the larger black and brown communities of our nation in low regard but is willing to carve out exceptions for those who make some whites sufficiently comfortable? We now have our answer to that question, if we're willing to examine it. But one thing about which we should be clear as we conduct that examination is this: the election of Barack Obama was not the result of a national evolution to a truly antiracist consciousness or institutional praxis. And this we know for reasons we shall now explore.

SAME AS IT EVER WAS: BARACK OBAMA AND THE PROBLEM OF WHITE DENIAL

That white folks would find it tempting, in light of Obama's mass appeal and his ascent to the presidency, to declare the struggle against racism over should surprise no one.

As we'll see below, even when the system of racism and white supremacy was more firmly entrenched, white folks by and large failed to see what all the fuss was about. So needless to say, with Barack Obama now in the nation's top political position, it is to be expected that once again white America would point to such a thing as firm confirmation that all was right with the world. Indeed, the day after Obama's victory, the *Wall Street Journal* editorial page intoned: "One promise of his victory is that perhaps we can put to rest the myth of racism as a barrier to achievement in this splendid country."[3]

In fact, even before Obama had been declared the winner of the election, proclamations of racism's early death were becoming ubiquitous. And so, ten days before the vote, columnist Frank Rich, writing in the *New York Times*, declared that concerns about white racism possibly sinking Obama's ship were so obviously absurd as to indicate evidence of "prevailing antiwhite bias" on the part of the media types who continually raised the subject. He went on to explain that white America's distrust of blacks "crumbles when they actually get to know specific black people."[4] Though Rich's point about the willingness of whites to open up to individual blacks once they become familiar with them may be true for many, he, like most commentators, ignores the fact that most black folks will not get the chance to be known in this way by the average white person. As such, to proclaim a phenomenon observable in the presidential race (whites, getting to know Obama and choosing him in the voting booth) as common or likely to obtain in everyday situations and encounters seems a bit far-fetched.

Then there was columnist Richard Cohen, who said in the *Washington Post* on the morning of the election, "It is not just that he (Obama) is post-racial; so is the nation he is generationally primed to lead," and then closed his piece by suggesting, in a bizarre appropriation of civil rights movement language, "we have overcome."[5]

On a personal note, about a week before the election I received an e-mail from a young white man who proclaimed his desire for Obama to win so that the nation would finally be able to "stop talking about racism, and move on to more important subjects," and so that "blacks would have to stop whining about discrimination, and focus on pulling themselves up by their bootstraps instead."

On election eve, before Obama had accumulated enough electoral votes to be proclaimed the winner, former New York City mayor (and Republican presidential candidate) Rudy Giuliani had made clear what an Obama victory would mean for the nation. Speaking of what appeared at that moment to be a sure Obama win, Giuliani noted that if the trend at that point in the evening held up, "we've achieved history tonight and we've moved beyond . . . the whole idea of race and racial separation and unfairness."[6] Interestingly, not only did none of the other commentators challenge Giuliani's formulation, but they also failed to note the obvious irony of his comment. Namely, if an Obama win by necessity would indicate the veritable death of racism in the United States, then would an Obama loss have suggested deeply entrenched bigotry in the eyes of Giuliani and others making the same argument? Had McCain won, could we have expected these prophets of achieved color blindness to condemn their fellow voters for being so obviously racist as to vote against a black man? After all, if voting for Obama means people have put away racism, by definition, voting against him would have to mean they had not, right? Actually no, of course, but such a conclusion is where arguments like that of Giuliani necessarily lead.

In truth, such a proposition (that the victory of one person of color signifies a victory over racism aimed at nearly 90 million) is very nearly the definition of lunacy. And note, it is the kind of proposition one would never make regarding sexism in a place like Pakistan, just because Benazir Bhutto was twice elected prime minister of the place; or in India, Israel, or Great Britain, by virtue of all three having elected women as the heads of their respective states. Surely, had Hillary Clinton captured the nomination of her party and gone on to win in November, no one with even a scintilla of common sense would have argued that a result such as this signaled the obvious demise of sexism in the United States. But that is essentially what so many would have us believe to be true of racism, thanks to the national effort that elected Barack Obama.

What white America has apparently missed, in spite of all the Black History Month celebrations to which we have lately been exposed, is that there have always been individually successful persons of color. Their pictures adorn the walls of our elementary school classrooms; their stories get told, albeit in an abbreviated and sanitized way, every February, when corporations and the Ad Council take to the airwaves to tell us about so-and-so great black inventor, or so-and-so great black artist, or so-and-so great black literary giant. What remains unsaid, but which forms the background noise of all this annual praise for the triumphs of black Americans (or, at other times, Latinos and Latinas, Asian-Pacific Americans, or the continent's indigenous persons), is the systematic oppression that marked the society at the time when most of their achievements transpired. In other words, even in the midst of crushing oppression these hearty souls managed to find a way out of no way, as the saying goes. But that hardly suggests that their singular achievements, even multiplied hundreds of times over, actually rendered the system any less oppressive for all the rest. Thus, Madame C.J. Walker managed to become a millionaire developing and selling beauty products to black women in 1911. This achievement, though of importance in the history of American entrepreneurship, and to the narrative of black success, nonetheless fails to alter the fact that, on balance, 1911 was not a good year to be black in the United States, Madame Walker notwithstanding. Though I am hardly so naïve as to suggest that nothing has changed since 1911, the point still holds: the triumph of individuals of color cannot, in itself, serve as proof of widespread systemic change.

Although it is possible that the political success of Barack Obama could serve to open the minds of whites as to the potentiality of effective black leadership, it is also possible that it might deepen the denial in which so much of the white public has been embedded for generations. And although Obama's success has had a measurable effect on young men and women of color, who appear empowered by his example—and this could lead to greater levels of accomplishment for still more persons of color, thereby producing a ripple effect when it comes to collective racial uplift—it is also possible that this sense of pride may be stalled if Obama is unable to deliver on his promise of "Change We Can Believe In," thanks to the exigencies of Washington politics. Long story short, what the rise of Obama comes to mean, regarding race or any other subject, remains to be seen.

But what we can say, without fear of contradiction, is that it does not signify, as some would have it, a fundamental diminution of institutional racism in the United States at present. Contrary to the proclamations of conservatives, both white and of color—such as Abigail Thernstrom and Ward Connerly, who have been among the chief critics and organized opponents of affirmative action programs since the mid-1990s—Obama's ability to attract white votes (and even then, let us remember, a minority of those) hardly suggests that we can put away various civil rights remedies and proclaim opportunities to be truly open and equitable. That white America may desperately want Obama's success to serve as the final nail in the political coffin of civil rights activism—and even the media seems to have evinced this hope, as with the August 2008 *New York Times* article that asked whether Obama marks the "end of black politics" altogether—hardly speaks to whether it should be used as that nail, or whether there is evidence to support the notion that his individual victories are proxies for institutional transformation.[7]

Though the evidence about our nation's progress says something else altogether, it turns out that white folks have never paid much attention to the evidence, and so denial has long carried the day. This, of course, is no shock in 2009. After all, it is not only the age of Obama, but the age of Oprah Winfrey, Denzel Washington, Colin Powell, Tiger Woods, the Williams sisters, J-Lo, Jackie Chan, Lucy Liu, Russell Simmons, P. Diddy, and any number of dizzyingly successful folks of color in the worlds of entertainment, sports, and politics. Hip-hop is, for most youth of whatever race, at least part of the sound track of their lives. With such apparent signs of progress, who can blame white folks for thinking the work has been done, and that it is now time to move on to other subjects, leaving the stale topic of racism in the dustbin of history?

Given such a transformation of popular culture as we have seen in the past few decades, it should hardly surprise us to read that according to a summer 2008 Gallup/ *USA Today* poll, more than three in four whites say that blacks have "just as good a chance as whites to get any job for which they are qualified" (a proposition with which fewer than half of African Americans agree). Likewise, it can't be much of a shock to learn that 80 percent of whites polled say blacks have "just as good a chance as whites to get a good education," while fewer than half of blacks agree. Or that 85 percent of whites claim blacks have "just as good a chance to get any housing they can afford," while only 52 percent of blacks agree. Or that only about a third of whites accept the proposition that discrimination has played a major role in producing income disparities between whites and blacks.[8] Or that, according to a survey for CNN and *Essence* magazine, only one in nine whites believe racial discrimination against blacks is still a very serious problem, while nearly four times that many say it's not a serious problem at all.[9] And all this, despite a July 2008 *New York Times*/CBS poll, in which seven in ten blacks said they had suffered a specific discriminatory incident (up from 62 percent who said this in 2000).[10] No, there is nothing particularly surprising about any of this.

The outward trappings of major transformative change appear to be everywhere, causing whites and blacks both, in the wake of Obama's victory, to announce their hope and expectations that race relations will improve in coming years.[11] So white denial (and perhaps even a bit from persons of color themselves) makes sense. It fits the visuals beamed into our living rooms, incomplete as they are.

But as predictable as this denial may be today—and however maddening it must be to the persons of color whose very sanity and judgment, indeed life experiences are being called into question by such denial—it is far more enraging to realize that the inability or unwillingness of white America to see racial discrimination as a problem is a pathology with a lengthy and disturbing pedigree. Putting aside the fact that, as with the examples above, we seem to be able to name all the really powerful black and brown folks on a couple of hands—and this, one might suggest, indicates that they are, by definition, exceptions to a much different-looking rule—the bigger problem with white denial is that it isn't a modern malady.

Though whites may now be seeking to use Obama as evidence of racism's eradication, let us remember that long before he burst onto the national scene—indeed, even at a time when he was an infant, well before anyone could have foreseen what he would become, and even before the passage of modern civil rights legislation—white Americans were fairly nonchalant about the problems facing persons of color, choosing in most cases to deny what all their senses (and surely their eyes, fixed on the television as most already were by the early 1960s) had to be telling them: that they were living in an apartheid nation; that theirs was no land of freedom and democracy, no oasis of liberty, but rather a formal white supremacy, a racially fascistic state for millions of people.

And so, in 1963, roughly two-thirds of whites told Gallup pollsters that blacks were treated equally in white communities. Even more along the lines of delusion, in 1962, nearly 90 percent of whites said black children were treated equally in terms of educational opportunity.[12] All of which is to say that in August 1963, as 200,000 people marched on Washington, and as they stood there in the sweltering heat, listening to Dr. Martin Luther King Jr.'s famous "I Have a Dream" speech, most whites seeing the news that evening were, in effect, thinking to themselves, what's the problem, exactly? Dream? Why dream? Everything is just fine now. Isn't it?

Or consider the 1950s, and the way in which white denial manifested so prominently among the very persons who had been most implicated in the maintenance of white domination. So, for instance, when racist forces in Congress issued their "Southern Manifesto" in response to Supreme Court rulings invalidating racially separate schools, they noted with no apparent misgiving that the push for desegregation was "destroying the amicable relations between the white and Negro races that have been created through 90 years of patient effort by the good people of both races. It has planted hatred and suspicion where there has been heretofore friendship and understanding."[13]

Although modern polling techniques weren't in place in the 1930s one can imagine few whites at that time seeing racism and the oppression of black people as a major concern. Likewise, even at the height of overt white supremacist rule in the United States—during the 1890s, as Black Codes and massive violence against post-emancipation blacks were reaching their zenith[14]—one can read editorials in newspapers all around the South in which it was proclaimed how well whites and blacks got along, and how everything would be just fine if those "yankees" would just stop messing with Dixie. And of course it was in the mid-nineteenth century that a well-respected physician of his day, Dr. Samuel Cartwright, opined that enslaved blacks occasionally ran away due to a mental illness, drapetomania, which apparently rendered them incapable of fully appreciating just how good they had it. In short, at no point in American history have whites, by and large, believed that folks of color were getting a raw deal. That we were wrong in every generation prior to the current one in holding such a rosy and optimistic view apparently gives most whites little pause. And so we continue to reject claims of racism as so much whining, as "playing the race card" or some such thing, never wondering, even for a second, how a bunch who have proven so utterly inept at discerning the truth for hundreds of years can at long last be trusted to accurately intuit other people's reality.

Of course, Obama's own tendency to de-emphasize racism and ongoing social injustice hasn't helped. It may have helped Obama's campaign, make no mistake. In fact, had he spoken with any regularity about the frightening reality of U.S. history and the legacy of racism today, there is little doubt that he'd never have found himself so much as a contender for the presidency, a subject about which I'll have more to say below. But as astute as the political judgment of Obama's campaign team may have been on these matters, the general avoidance of race as an issue on his part does tend to feed mainstream white denial.

THE EVIDENCE OF THINGS NOT SPOKEN: RACISM AND WHITE PRIVILEGE TODAY

And so it is worth taking note of all the things Barack Obama never mentioned on the campaign trail, but which confirm the salience of racism in the modern era. As a well-read, highly versed (and by his own admission, once racially obsessed) man of color, there is little chance that he fails to know any of the following, and yet he mentioned none of it, at least not in public.

Even after he was forced to address race in the wake of the dust-up over remarks made by his former pastor, Jeremiah Wright, Obama played it close to the vest, talking more about how the historic legacy of racism had shaped the contours of racial inequity and had fed the black anger expressed by Wright, which anger was seen as so threatening to much if not most of white America. By speaking in terms of past injuries and the lingering grievances generated by the same, Obama deftly managed to speak about racism without forcing white folks to confront just how real and how present-day the problem is. Sure, speaking of racism even in the past can be risky, especially when you mix it with any discussion of what our obligations are today to address the legacy of that racism. But to make an issue of ongoing racism and presently dispensed privilege—which, after all, would seem to implicate the current generation of white Americans more than is suggested by a backward-looking historical point—would have been infinitely more risky. It is one thing to note that the legacy of slavery, segregation, and other forms of racism has been a massive racial wealth gap—indeed, the typical white family today has about eleven times the net worth of the typical black family and eight times the net worth of the typical Latino/a family,[15] and much of this gap is directly traceable to a history of unequal access to capital[16] —but it is quite another to point out that this wealth gap continues to grow, not only because of past unequal opportunity, but also because of present-day institutional racism.

And so rather than speak of these matters, Obama avoided them, and when he did engage them, he did so in a way that tended to paper over the ongoing racial inequities that beset the nation, in favor of a narrative far preferred by white folks: the narrative of the color-blind society achieved, or at least, very nearly so. In his book, *The Audacity of Hope*, for instance, Obama speaks of the obstacles facing black and brown America as little different from those facing working-class and middle-class whites. To hear Obama tell it, all are in the same boat, and as he would explain during a speech in Selma, Alabama, during the campaign, the civil rights movement, or what he called the "Moses generation," had brought the nation 90 percent of the way to racial justice. It was now, according to Obama, time for the "Joshua generation" to carry the load the last tenth of the way.[17]

Income and Jobs

But in a land where the average black family has less than one-tenth the net worth of the average white family, and the average Latino family has about one-eighth as much, it's hard to square Obama's mathematical calculus of progress with the facts. So too when other data is considered, such as the fact that black high school graduates actually have higher unemployment rates than white dropouts;[18] or the fact that white men with college degrees earn, on average, a third more than similar black men;[19] or the fact that only 7 percent of private sector management jobs are held by African Americans, and another 7 percent by Latinos, while whites hold over 80 percent of all such positions;[20] or the fact that middle-class black families have to put in approximately 480 more hours per year—equal to twelve work weeks—relative to similar whites, just to make the same incomes as their middle-class white counterparts;[21] or the fact that blacks, Latinos, and Native North Americans are 2.5 to 3 times more likely than whites to be poor, while Asian Americans are about 30 percent more likely than whites to be poor.[22] In the case of Asians, higher poverty rates and lower incomes often remain the norm, despite higher, on average, educational attainment than whites', thanks to high-skilled immigration. And so, as one study of Asian mobility in Houston, Texas, discovered, although Asian Americans in Harris County are 50 percent more likely than whites in the county to have a college degree, they have considerably lower incomes and occupational status than the lesser-educated whites with whom they compete for opportunities.[23]

And given some of the data suggesting that things are getting worse for blacks—and in particular for black men—it is especially troubling to think that the public may come to believe the rhetoric about racial equity having been essentially achieved. So consider that at the same time America can make a black man president, data from the labor department indicates that for average young black men today, things are not nearly so rosy. Indeed, the typical young black male growing up today will earn 12 percent less than his father did a generation ago. Furthermore, the data suggests that while most middle-class white kids will grow up to do better, economically, than their parents did at the same age, most middle-class black kids will grow up to find themselves having fallen backwards and actually doing worse than their parents. Indeed, the numbers show that black youth from solidly middle-class families are nearly three times as likely as similar whites to fall to the bottom of the income distribution, and nearly half of all black middle-class youth will do so.[24]

Naturally some will suggest that this data, however troubling it may be, has little to do with institutional racism in the United States today. Perhaps non-discriminatory factors such as differential qualification levels, unequal educational backgrounds, or family composition could explain economic disparities between whites and people of color. But while it is true that earnings disparities, wealth gaps, and differences in occupational status are not only the result of racism perpetrated by whites, the evidence that discrimination contributes to the phenomenon indicated by the data is strong. Even after controlling for such ostensibly race-neutral factors as differential test scores and grades, family background, and other variables that can impact income levels, white males still receive about 17 percent more than their otherwise identical black male counterparts.[25] But beyond mere income disparity data, direct evidence of ongoing racial discrimination is also plentiful, however much President Obama may have finessed it on the campaign trail.

So what does it say about how much we've transcended race, or rather, failed to do so, that according to a study from just a few years ago, conducted by economists at MIT and the University of Chicago, job applicants with white-sounding names are 50 percent more likely to be called back for a job interview than applicants with black-sounding names, even when all relevant qualifications and experience are indistinguishable?[26] Or that, according to the same study, for black-named applicants to have an equal chance at a callback, they must actually have eight more years of experience than those with white names? One thing it surely says, but which has gone unremarked upon by most pundits, and which remained unspoken in the presidential campaign, is that white fears about so-called "reverse discrimination" are based on irrational and nonsensical delusion. After all, if it were really white folks who couldn't catch a break when looking for a job, then a study such as this would have come to the exact opposite conclusion of what it actually found. When the researchers sent out the résumés to prospective employers, it would have been all the "Tamikas" and "Jamals" who got called in by enthusiastic companies bent on hiring black folks, and it would have been the "Connors" and "Beckys" left out in the cold to wonder what in the world had gone wrong. But this didn't happen, because it never does. And yet, not only did Obama not speak this fundamental truth—that it is still very much the usual suspects who face the obstacles of race-based discrimination—rather, he pandered to the lie in his Philadelphia speech on race, wherein he mentioned, as though it were perfectly valid, white anger over losing out on a position because of a preference given to a minority.[27]

What does it say that, according to another study conducted by Princeton sociology professor Devah Pager, white males with a criminal record are more likely than black males without one to be called back for a job interview, even when all credentials, experience, demeanor, and communication and dress style are the same between them?[28] Or that according to a massive national study conducted by legal scholars Alfred and Ruth Blumrosen, who examined tens of thousands of businesses, at least one-third of all employers in the nation are racially biased and discriminate regularly against job applicants of color, and at least 1.3 million black and brown job-seekers will face racial bias during their job search in a given year?[29] Other research would suggest far higher rates of discrimination than even the Blumrosen study was able to find. So, for instance, according to data from the mid-1990s, compiled by the Office of Federal Contract Compliance Programs, as many as three-fourths of all businesses covered by civil rights and affirmative action laws were in "substantial violation" of those laws, because of ongoing discrimination against persons of color and women of all colors.[30]

What about the fact that according to study after study for years—not to mention a healthy dose of common sense—most jobs, especially the most lucrative ones, aren't filled based on qualifications anyway, or open competition, so much as by networking and word-of-mouth? And what of the racial impact of this truth: namely, that it is disproportionately folks of color who end up "out of the loop" when it comes to such networks, thereby scratched from the start of the race and afforded less opportunity to demonstrate their abilities.[31] Indeed it is the matter of social and professional networking that explains, in large measure, why persons of color with the same educational background as whites, and of the same age, doing the same job, so often earn much less.[32] So, for instance, a recent study found that Chinese Americans in the legal and medical professions earn, on average, about 44 percent less than their white counterparts, despite equal qualifications and educational attainment.[33] Whereas white job-seekers are able to access more lucrative positions, be they professional, managerial, or even blue-collar, thanks to the networks within which they so often find themselves, black and brown Americans, equally qualified as their white counterparts, have to take positions with less capitalized firms and companies, with the resultant lower pay, because they simply aren't in a position to network with the right people. Although this form of exclusion is not illegal, it does amount to institutional racism—a kind of racism that is perpetuated within structural settings, even without deliberate and bigoted intent, due to the normal workings of long-entrenched policies, practices, and procedures. And for whites, the privileges that flow from the arrangement are substantial.

Surely the old boys' network (and the institutional racism embedded within it) explains the ongoing disparities in the awarding of government contracts to private businesses. Currently, about 92 percent of all municipal, state, and federal contracts are awarded to white-owned firms.[34] This result is not necessarily, or even likely, the result of overt racial bias; rather, it flows naturally from the way in which networking and connections are so central to the process of contracting and subcontracting. If a white-owned firm has subcontracts to offer, they will be most likely to turn to those smaller firms (also white-owned) whom they know, rather than to include black-, Latino-, Asian- or Native American–owned businesses, even when the latter may be capable of doing equally good or even better work, simply because they are less likely to know of such firms to begin with.

In all, it is estimated that African American workers alone lose over $120 billion in wages each year thanks to labor market discrimination of one kind or another: monies they would be paid if opportunity were truly equal, but which they do not in fact receive, much to their detriment, and much to the benefit of the mostly white employers for whom they work, and who get to retain the unpaid amount in their own coffers.[35]

Housing

Or consider the arena of housing. Although much attention has been paid to the overall housing crisis in America, little of that attention has examined the way in which racial discrimination continues to limit where persons of color can live, and on what terms. On the one hand, of course, there is a long and pernicious history of race-based housing discrimination, which has culminated in many of the racially separate residential patterns we see today. From restrictive covenants that prohibited families of color from purchasing property in most white neighborhoods, to overt violence against people of color seeking to move into formerly white space, to efforts like the FHA and VA loan programs, which for the first thirty years operated in a blatantly discriminatory manner, people of color have been deliberately deprived of assets, net worth, and housing equity that so many millions of whites have been able to take for granted. This history, the effects of which are transmitted intergenerationally (since assets or the decided lack thereof are typically handed down to one's children and grandchildren), has deprived people of color of hundreds of billions of dollars in housing equity over the years.[36]

But in addition to these accumulated disadvantages of the past—which Barack Obama actually has discussed, albeit briefly, in his speech on race delivered in Philadelphia on March 18, 2008—there are also significant barriers to equal housing opportunity today, which constitute still more evidence of the salience of race in twenty-first-century America. Indeed, according to recently released federal estimates, 2006 actually witnessed the largest number of housing discrimination complaints (including race-based complaints) on record.[37] Despite federal fair-housing laws, on the books since 1968, there was virtually no enforcement mechanism in place to make the law meaningful for nearly a quarter-century, and private studies have long estimated that there are at least 2 million instances of racial discrimination in housing each year, ranging from outright bias in mortgage lending or rental markets to more subtle forms, such as "steering" buyers or renters to certain neighborhoods, based on race and whether they'll "fit in."[38] Other estimates place the number of race–based housing discrimination incidents as high as 3.7 million per year.[39] One study in 2001, which sent out matched and paired "testers" to look for rental housing in Houston, found that discrimination occurred in 80 percent of all rental attempts by black testers.[40]

When it comes to persons looking to purchase a home, research has found that lenders often provide less detailed loan information to black customers than to whites, are quicker to urge blacks to seek loans elsewhere, and are more likely to discourage black loan seekers by telling them how complicated and time-consuming the application process might be.[41] Additionally, according to data uncovered under the Home Mortgage Disclosure Act, while blacks and whites with excellent credit appear to be treated equally, there is a substantial gap between the way whites and blacks with questionable credit are treated by the banking industry. As the *Wall Street Journal* reported in 1995, nearly 70 percent of whites with poor credit are able to receive a mortgage, compared to only 16 percent of blacks with equally poor credit.[42]

And as the nation is increasingly introduced to the workings of the subprime lending market, let us not ignore the particularly racial component of the mess. As several studies have shown, banks often reject applicants of color, even when they have credit records similar to whites with the same incomes. Then, these rejected applicants turn to secondary or subprime lenders, often owned by the very banks that turned them down (or which are subsidized by them in the form of credit lines), and which specialize in loans to persons who can't otherwise get financing. These subprime lenders then charge far higher interest than the banks that originally rejected the supposedly high-risk applicant. By doing so, the lenders make huge profits and place borrowers in jeopardy by driving up the amount they must repay, thereby increasing the likelihood of default, late payments, missed payments, and even foreclosure. Since the originators of the subprime loans (most often independent mortgage brokers, rather than regulated institutions such as banks) typically sell the loans to larger investors almost immediately after the paperwork is signed, they have little incentive to keep costs down for the borrower, since, if the borrower defaults, the lender, having already dumped the loan, will suffer no loss as a result.

A recent study of Citigroup (which includes Citi, the group's subprime lender) found that Citi in North Carolina charged higher interest even to borrowers who could have qualified for regular loans. In the process, more than 90,000 mostly black borrowers were roped into predatory loans, and as a result paid an average of $327 more per month for mortgages than those getting loans from a prime lender. This added up to over $110,000 in excess payments over the life of the loans, on average.[43] And at the same time that banks are steering blacks with good credit to subprime lenders, whites with good credit who apply for loans with subprime lenders are routinely referred to prime lenders, who offer loans at lower interest rates. Evidence from one sizable study in 2000 indicated that blacks, Latinos, Asian Americans, and indigenous persons all pay higher mortgage rates, on average, than white borrowers, even when income, debt load, and several measures of credit history are the same.[44] Likewise, even high-income blacks are targeted for higher-cost loans, so that upper-income black families in black-majority neighborhoods are three times more likely than low-income white borrowers to have subprime, high-risk instruments for their home mortgages.[45]

The collective impact of this housing bias is enormous. Most obviously, it deprives families of color of billions of dollars in lost potential wealth and assets. Studies place the cost of present-day housing discrimination at over $4 billion annually for people of color, and further estimate that today's black communities have been deprived of nearly half a trillion dollars in wealth due to past and present housing discrimination in the United States.[46] White folks should probably think about that the next time they feel like complaining about black folks soaking up government money or "looking for a handout," since these numbers suggest the real problem is the way folks of color have been collectively denied equity and wealth that they had earned and to which they are entitled.

Education

Consider education. Even as much is made of America's "failing" schools and the often significant racial achievement gaps between whites on the one hand, and blacks and Latinos on the other, little attention is given to the way in which the policies, practices, and procedures within schools often perpetuate those racial inequities and even make them worse.

To begin with, and in part related to the ongoing de facto housing segregation patterns so common in the nation, students of color start out with substantial disadvantages relative to whites. The average black student, for instance, attends a school with twice as many low-income students as the typical white youth,[47] and schools that are mostly attended by black and Latino students are more than ten times as likely as mostly white schools to be schools with concentrated levels of student poverty.[48] In fact, even black kids with family incomes higher than those of whites are more likely to attend concentrated poverty schools.[49] This concentration of poverty in black and brown schools magnifies any number of social problems within the school environment, including inadequate nutrition and health care, family crises like long-term unemployment, and the emotional and material toll of growing up in marginalized spaces cut off from access to the social and professional networks so important to success among middle- and upper-middle-class families. It isn't that black and brown kids need to sit next to white kids in order to learn—and indeed, anyone who supports integration for such a "rub-off" purpose is guilty of crass and paternalistic racism—but simply that when kids who are poor are crammed in buildings, given the impression that they don't count (because they know they don't have the resources that exist in suburban and private schools), and then expected to learn and achieve at the same level as the kids in the neighborhoods that are economically viable, they figure out the game pretty quickly, and then proceed to fulfill every prophecy about them already held by far too many in the adult population.

Then, as if access and privileges denied to students of color—and, on the flip side, the advantages enjoyed by whites—weren't bad enough, schools serving mostly white and affluent students are able to spend considerably more, on average, per pupil than schools serving mostly lower-income students of color. In large measure, the financial imbalance stems from the principal funding mechanisms for education, such as property tax revenues, which result in more affluent areas having more to spend than working-class and poor communities. Even additional funding from state government to make up for the property tax shortfalls can't equalize opportunity: at best, such efforts result in formal parity, but given the greater challenges facing lower-income neighborhoods and the inability of poor families to kick in additional monies for the operation of their schools (something that is taken for granted in communities where affluent families live), this parity exists in name only. In practice, the funding gap, relative to need, remains substantial: on the order of roughly a thousand dollars per pupil, per year, between schools serving mostly white children and those serving mostly students of color.[50] With fewer per-pupil resources, such schools then have a harder time attracting highly skilled and qualified teachers, which has an especially pernicious impact on student learning. In fact, high-poverty schools (disproportionately serving a large number of students of color) have, on average, three times as many uncertified teachers, or teachers who are teaching outside of their field of study, as teachers serving low-poverty and mostly white schools.[51]

Predictably, those on the right argue that money doesn't matter, and that what really makes the difference to a child's education is personal motivation. Yet one might take note of just how insincere such arguments sound, coming from people whose every other move in life is predicated on the notion that money does matter, and that it matters quite a lot. After all, these are the same folks who tell us they need tax cuts, so they can keep more of their money, presumably because it matters, and will lead to greater levels of investment and "trickle-down" benefits for all. These are folks who read the daily stock reports, presumably because money matters (and they want to know how much they have every single day). These are folks who send their kids to outrageously expensive schools if they can afford to do so. Either this means that money does indeed matter, or it suggests that persons such as this are ridiculously wasteful with their resources, squandering tens of thousands of dollars each year when they could do just as well sending their children to the public school down the street. Unless those who claim money doesn't matter decide to shut down their prep schools, forswear tutors and test prep classes for their kids, and announce to the world that they will be shuttling their children off to community college in lieu of the Ivy League—since, after all, why waste all that money?—the rest of us should probably remain skeptical of their assurances that money doesn't make much difference in the education of children.

Of course it's true that money or the lack thereof isn't the only issue. Additionally, there is the matter of how teacher expectations influence student outcomes, and how these expectations are often tied to race and class stereotypes. It is commonly believed, for instance, that blacks and Latinos are not as committed as whites to education and academic achievement, this despite multiple studies showing it is whites who manifest the most cynicism and nonchalance about doing well in school, and that black students are every bit as academically inclined and motivated as their white counterparts.[52] As a result of the stereotypes however, which persist despite the evidence to counter them, teachers and counselors end up assigning students to certain classes—honors or advanced placement, standard, or remedial level—based more on their own internalized biases about student ability than on anything objective. Black and Latino students, nationwide, are about half as likely as whites to be found in upper-level classes and twice as likely to be in remedial classes. Even when their prior performance would justify higher placement, students of color are still significantly less likely to be given honors or advanced-placement opportunities than whites, even when the latter have lower grades or test scores.[53] Partly this is due to educator bias, but it is also in part the result of systemic inequity: schools serving mostly white students have about three times as many advanced level courses offered as schools serving mostly students of color. Thus, even in the total absence of racial bias on the part of school officials, the lack of certain course offerings deprives capable and hard-working students of color of equal opportunity with their white counterparts.[54] Evidence then suggests that children who are tracked lower tend to suffer a downward spiral in terms of performance, in part because of a lowered sense of self-efficacy, in part because of not being challenged, and in part because of their own withdrawal from work they find stultifying and meaningless, unlike the more engaging curricula offered to those—mostly whites—in the advanced-level courses.[55]

Then, in a move that certainly contributes to glaring racial inequities in higher education, colleges tend to over-rely on standardized tests such as the SAT and ACT, even as these instruments have been deemed inadequate to the task of truly selecting more qualified students, and have proven time and again to disproportionately limit opportunities for students of color, who, through no fault of their own, haven't been exposed to the same material and degree of instruction as most whites.[56]

Beyond course offerings and the inequity generated by certain forms of testing, there is also widespread disparity in terms of school discipline. As Indiana University's Russell Skiba has found after examining years of research on school disciplinary actions, students of color are considerably more likely than whites to be suspended or expelled, even though there is no statistically significant difference between the rates at which white students and students of color break serious school rules, for which such punishment could be the result.[57] Although most Americans appear to believe that black and Latino students have far higher rates of drug possession, or weapons possession, or fights in school, over a decade's worth of data from the Department of Education suggests otherwise: in most years, racial differences in fighting are not dramatic; whites are equally or more likely to use or possess drugs, alcohol, or cigarettes on campus; and whites are equally or more likely to carry a weapon to school.[58] Yet because of racial stereotypes, it is students of color who are suspected of these things and therefore searched, detected, and punished.

Not to mention, as Skiba explains, the disparate punishment that is especially a problem for offenses at the lower end of the seriousness spectrum. So while teachers may respond to rude or disrespectful in-class behavior by whites with a warning or a call to parents—because they are less likely to view such children as irredeemable threats to their safety and classroom order—the same behavior by students of color is regularly met with referral to the principal's office. And with enough referrals, suspension or expulsion typically becomes mandatory. So racially biased perception leads to initially disparate discipline, which then is followed by disparity at greater levels of discipline, which then not only reinforces the stereotypes that gave rise to the disparate punishment, but also breeds frustration and resentment among students of color. This frustration is then directly correlated with a withdrawal of academic effort, followed by a greater risk of academic failure, which is then followed by greater likelihood of economic hardship and even criminal activity in later years. By allowing racially disparate discipline to continue, the nation's educators literally create a school-to-prison pipeline, by virtue of marking certain kids as "bad" before they are even in high school in many cases. In such a setting as this, education becomes less a liberating force than one that reinscribes existing hierarchies of domination and subordination, less a "great equalizer" as it is often called, and more a terrible unequalizer for millions of youth of color across the nation.

Criminal Justice and the Law

Or consider the criminal justice system, perhaps the one arena of national life where racial disparities are most stark, and where evidence of unequal treatment is the most dramatic. In 1964, just three years after Barack Obama was born, about two-thirds of all persons locked up in the nation's jails and prisons were white, while a third were persons of color, mostly African American. By the early 1990s, those numbers had essentially flip-flopped, so that today, nearly two-thirds of persons locked up are persons of color while only a third are white,[59] a number that has persisted into the twenty-first century.[60]

There are only two possible theories to explain this inversion of incarceration data. The first would be that sometime around 1965, white folks awoke from a deep criminal slumber, in which sleepwalking state we had been committing all kinds of crimes, and said to ourselves that the time had come to retire from our criminal endeavors. Corollary to this theory, one would also have to imagine that around the same time, black and brown folks, hearing the news that whites were getting out of the crime business, decided to fill the gap left open by the white decision to walk the straight and narrow. In other words, white folks shaped up, while folks of color went on a criminal spree unparalleled in the history of humankind. The second theory would be that although the percentages of crime committed by whites or by folks of color remained roughly the same throughout this period, law enforcement resources tilted heavily in favor of catching, prosecuting, and incarcerating people of color. Indeed, a look at the evidence makes quite clear that the latter is far and away more accurate than the former as an explanation.

Nowhere is this truer than with regard to the so-called war on drugs: so-called because rarely is the war fought on the front lines of where the drugs actually are. Contrary to popular perception—so popular that when asked to envision a drug user, upwards of 95 percent of whites say they picture a black person[61]—most drug users are white, and indeed, on a per capita basis, whites actually have an equal or higher rate of use than either African Americans or Latinos.[62] This means that if you were to randomly drug test 1,000 whites, 1,000 blacks, and 1,000 Latinos, in most years you would end up with at least as many, if not more "hits" in the white group. This is especially true among the young, where drug use is typically far higher among whites than youth of color.[63] And yet, when it comes to who is being searched, arrested, prosecuted, and incarcerated for drug activity, the picture looks far different than the usage rates would justify. So, in spite of whites comprising more than seven in ten drug users, and despite blacks and Latinos combined representing less than 25 percent of all users, the latter comprise nearly 90 percent of all persons locked up in a given year for a drug possession offense, while whites represent less than 10 percent of drug possession incarcerations annually.[64] Nationally, black youth are forty-eight times more likely than whites to be incarcerated for a first-time drug offense, even when all factors surrounding the crime are the same.[65] In all, black drug users are nearly twenty times more likely than anyone else to spend time in prison for their use, and in fifteen states, the rate of black incarceration for drug offenses is anywhere from twenty to fifty-seven times greater than for whites, despite equal or greater rates of drug law violations by whites.[66] When all other factors surrounding an arrest are the same, black cocaine offenders are twice as likely to be sent to prison and will serve, on average, forty months more than white offenders.[67]

Partly, the disproportionate incarceration of folks of color for drugs stems from the racially biased practices of law enforcement in terms of who is searched in the first place. According to Justice Department reports dating back almost a decade, black and Latino motorists are far more likely than whites to have their vehicles stopped and searched for illegal contraband, even though whites, when searched, are typically more likely to be found with drugs or other illegal items in our possession.[68] Likewise, a study by the General Accounting Office early in the decade found that although black women were nine times more likely than white women to be searched for drugs coming through airport customs checkpoints, white women were roughly twice as likely to actually be caught with drugs in their possession![69] Most recently, a study of stops and searches by the Los Angeles Police Department (LAPD) found that blacks are three times more likely than whites in L.A. to be stopped by police, and significant racial disparities remain even after things like differential crime rates and neighborhood demographics are taken into consideration. Interestingly, those whites searched by the LAPD were actually more likely to be found with drugs or other illegal items in their possession, suggesting that cops there have a higher threshold for suspicion when observing whites, and are quicker to suspect people of color, on much weaker evidence or probable cause. In all, blacks frisked by police were 42 percent less likely to be found with a weapon than whites, while Latinos frisked were a third less likely to have a weapon on them. In consent searches, blacks were one-fourth less likely to have drugs in their possession than whites, while Latinos were a third less likely to possess narcotics.[70]

In other words, racial profiling is real, it's racist, and it's not particularly intelligent as a method of law enforcement. At least, that would be the case if the purpose of the war on drugs were really to get drugs off the street. But given the apparent ineptitude with which the battle has been waged, one has to seriously wonder if that were ever really the purpose at all.

So too with racial profiling of Arabs and Muslims (or those thought to be either) in the wake of the terrorist attacks of September 11, 2001—another issue that received no attention whatsoever during the 2008 presidential campaign. Although many have suggested such profiling is rational, and indeed something of a moral and practical imperative, in truth such a practice is bad law enforcement and inherently unfair. As a law enforcement tool, so-called terrorist profiling based on perceived geographic origin or religious background is likely to fail. Al Qaeda, for instance, is active in several dozen nations, and many of its operatives would not fit a particular profile in terms of appearance. Furthermore, people conspiring to commit acts of terrorism would know the profile and work hard to go around it, while law enforcement would be so focused on one type of threat they might well let down their guard to other dangers. As for fairness, such profiling is obviously both racially and religiously selective. After all, no such calls for profiling emerged in the wake of terrorist acts by white Americans, such as the bombing of the Oklahoma City Federal Building by Tim McVeigh and Terry Nichols in 1995, or after the two decades of bombings by the Una-bomber, Theodore Kaczynski, or after the Olympic Park bombings of 1996 in Atlanta, carried out by Eric Rudolph, or after the more than 200 bombings or arsons at family planning and abortion clinics in North America since the mid-1970s.[71] That persons of Arab, Persian, North African, or South Asian descent, and others presumed to be terrorists because of the color of their skin, their accents, or their perceived religious beliefs, are currently facing such hostile treatment suggests that whatever progress may be signified by the victory of Barack Obama—Barack Hussein Obama no less—it has hardly translated into equitable treatment for all.[72]

Health Care

Moving on, consider health care. Although there was much talk during the 2008 presidential campaign about the lack of affordable coverage for more than 40 million Americans, little if any attention was paid, either by media or the candidates, to the emerging research as to the health consequences of racial discrimination. Likewise, when racial disparities were discussed, they were inevitably reduced to matters of economics—so, naturally, since folks of color are on balance poorer, they will suffer worse health outcomes—but the evidence of racially disparate health care provision was essentially ignored.

As regards this first matter, there have been dozens of studies in the last few years indicating that negative health outcomes for persons of color are highly and directly connected to experiences with racism perpetrated by whites: such experiences raise stress levels, leading to hypertension, which in turn is correlated with heart disease and other maladies.[73] Indeed, not only are hypertension gaps between whites and blacks widened by black experiences with racism, they appear to be related far more to racism than to economics. And so, as evolutionary biologist Joseph Graves has noted, when whites and blacks at the highest levels of income are excluded from hypertension data, racial disparities between the two groups entirely disappear.[74] This means those gaps manifest exclusively due to the experiences of affluent blacks; and among those experiences, one would have to include their constant awareness of the potential for being viewed through the lens of a racist stereotype, their real experiences with racist mistreatment (as chronicled in several volumes),[75] and the daily struggle of continually having to prove themselves—especially when they have managed to obtain a measure of success—in a society where racism remains quite prevalent.

As for the second issue, access to care, even when health care is available, studies have found that doctors are less likely to order a full range of diagnostic tests and treatments for black patients than for whites, even when these patients' finances and insurance coverage are comparable to their white counterparts.[76] Even when comparing blacks and whites of comparable age, sex, severity of disease, geographic location, and other factors that could influence the quality of medical treatment, blacks are 60 percent less likely to receive a coronary angioplasty or bypass surgery to relieve a serious heart condition, for example.[77] And as one study found, doctors presented with identical patient histories and symptoms overwhelmingly refer whites for more advanced treatment. According to the study, which presented doctors with videotaped interviews featuring actors trained to pose as patients with identical medical histories and symptoms, doctors were far less likely to refer black women for aggressive treatment of cardiac symptoms than white women. When asked to give their impression of the actors (whom they believed to be real patients), doctors routinely said they perceived the black "patients" as less intelligent, less likely to follow doctor's recommendations and thus cooperate with a treatment regimen, and more likely to miss appointments: this despite the fact that the actors had made identical comments and had presented identical symptoms.[78]

Additionally, studies have long demonstrated a direct linkage between the percentage of persons of color and low-income persons in a neighborhood, and the likelihood of the community being the location of a hazardous waste site or industrial facility that contaminates the surrounding air and water. This exposure then inflates the risk of disease for persons living in those communities, including the risk for cancer, asthma, and lead poisoning, the latter of which can directly impair cognitive function.[79] Although these waste sites and plants are likely not placed in these communities deliberately to harm persons of color—rather, they are likely sited there because of the lower cost of doing so and the relative political weakness of the persons in the community, who lack the clout to block such actions—the consequences are hardly different for lack of intentionality.

Yet, during a 2007 AFL-CIO forum in Las Vegas, candidate Obama demonstrated little desire to tackle directly the issue of racial disparities in health. When asked about health care for minorities, Obama spoke not of discrimination, or the way that toxic dumps and incinerators or lead-infested buildings predominate in black and brown communities, or the way that racism itself has contributed to the negative health outcomes experienced by millions of persons of color. Rather, he replied with an answer about the need for black people to have better nutrition, to eat less fast food, and to have better places to exercise:[80] all important to be sure, but hardly the key to reducing racial disparities in life expectancy, low birthweight, or infant mortality.

That such discrimination and widespread racial disparities as are documented above can exist and yet not become a campaign issue during a presidential race suggests how dangerous it is for politicians, especially those of color like Obama, to raise the subject. If honesty would result in an electoral smack-down (and make no mistake, it likely would), then honesty can conveniently and unceremoniously be relegated to the status of the proverbial illegitimate stepchild, passed over and regularly dissed on behalf of its favored sibling, which happens to be a lie—in this case, the lie of equal opportunity, one to which candidate Obama had little choice but to tether his campaign ship.

Racism, Hurricane Katrina, and the Post-Disaster Recovery

And it's a lie we seem compelled to keep repeating, even when the evidence of its deceptiveness is staring us in the face. So just three years after the world watched one of the great cities on Earth, New Orleans, nearly turned into a modern-day Atlantis, candidate Obama rarely discussed the veritable ethnic cleansing that has marked the post-Katrina rebuilding process. Oh yes, he mentioned Katrina, but only so as to make a point of the ineptitude of the Bush administration and its former FEMA chief—in other words, only insofar as mentioning it could score partisan political points by making the tragedy about corrupt and venal Republicans.

But nowhere did Obama discuss the decision at both the federal and state level, and by members of both parties, to prevent the Red Cross from entering the city to provide relief to people who were suffering for days without help.[81] Nowhere did he discuss the way in which mostly black New Orleanians were forced back across a bridge they were trying to cross to safety, blocked in their escape from the chaos by white sheriff's deputies from across the Mississippi river on the city's west bank. Nowhere did he discuss the way in which white tourists were rushed to the front of bus lines once relief came, while locals, mostly of color, had to wait. Nowhere did he discuss the rescue of approximately 7,000 whites in neighboring St. Bernard Parish by Orleans Parish school buses, even as 30,000 or more black folks languished in the heat of the convention center or Superdome.[82] Nowhere did he discuss the way in which Democrats and Republicans have conspired to tear down 5,000 units of perfectly usable public housing, or blocked any economic relief for renters in New Orleans for over a year. Indeed, as I write this, not a single person who was renting at the time of Katrina—people who are disproportionately of color, and certainly lower-income— has received a single penny from the $10 billion post-Katrina rebuilding program, known as the Road Home Community Development Block Grant: this compared to well over 100,000 homeowners, who are disproportionately white and affluent. Nowhere did he mention that after three years, of 10,000 rental units that had been projected to be rebuilt to house displaced persons of lower income, only 82 had been constructed as of summer 2008.[83]

That the purging of tens of thousands of lower-income black folks from New Orleans has happened, and yet there is no discussion at all of the blatant racism that has characterized so much of the city's rebuilding process is testament to how constrained candidates like Obama are as they seek national office. To discuss the racial implications of Katrina and its wake would be to bump up against the ever-present force of white denial: a force that led most whites, when polled three months after the event, to say that what had happened in New Orleans had no lessons at all to teach us about racial inequality in America.[84] To mention the evidence of widespread post-flood housing discrimination by white landlords, documented not only in Orleans Parish, but in surrounding mostly white parishes like Jefferson and St. Bernard,[85] would have been to signal a sympathy for the African American community that could only have damaged Obama's chances at victory in November. And so candidate Obama remained silent, and white denial went unchallenged. Indifference to the ongoing suffering of black New Orleanians—an indifference perpetuated by the silence of politicians, unwilling to clearly and accurately name what has been happening there—is, as Lance Hill, Executive Director of the Southern Institute for Education and Research has put it, the new face of racism in the twenty-first century. New or not, however, the impact is much the same as with deliberate injury. As Michael Eric Dyson explains:

> In a sense, if one conceives of racism as a cell phone,
> then active malice is the ring tone on its highest
> volume, while passive indifference is the ring tone
> on vibrate. In either case, whether loudly or silently,
> the consequence is the same: a call is transmitted, a
> racial message is communicated.[86]

In this case, the message being transmitted, of course, is that some lives are distinctly worth more than others, and that the algebra of relative importance does not favor the black and brown.

That anyone could deny the salience of race to the Katrina debacle is, of course stunning, especially as we have now learned that the reports of mass violence in the shelters—murders, rapes and molestations—were false. After all, to the extent the media reported on these claims of animalistic depravity without any proof, and to the extent white folks (and sadly, even lots of black and brown folks) believed the claims, without any proof at all, surely says something about race and racial inequality in America, does it not?[87] Surely it says that we are quick to believe the worst about poor black folks, in ways we never would were such absurd claims made about whites. Honestly, does anyone believe that if a hurricane took out Nantucket next year and someone started a rumor that whites were raping and killing people in the basement of the local Episcopal church, the media would report such a charge?

To ask the question is to answer it, and tells us all we really need to know about racism and its flip side, white privilege, in modern America.

Ironically, it was New Orleans-area whites, not blacks, who participated in the most disturbing post-Katrina violence. Although it was largely ignored at the time, false claims of mass black violence in the evacuation centers fed a siege mentality among the area's white population, which then precipitated real terrorism—including, it appears, several killings—by armed gangs. According to a December 2008 investigative report in *The Nation* magazine, as the floodwaters rose, residents in Algiers Point (a mostly white enclave on the city's west bank) began stockpiling weapons, including Uzis, and then, by their own admission, threatened blacks who they found in their neighborhood, including those who lived there. On several occasions, more than threats were issued.

Donnell Herrington, 29 at the time, lived about a mile from Algiers Point and was walking with his cousin and a friend through the area, hoping to reach the local ferry terminal where they could catch a bus out of town. A mob of whites who viewed any blacks in the community as interlopers shot at Herrington and hit him in the throat. As he got up and ran, a white gunman yelled after him, "Get him! Get that nigger!" The other two black men ran and were cornered by members of the mob who threatened to tie them up and burn them, but ultimately allowed them to flee if they promised to tell their friends not to set foot in the area again. Herrington, for his part, tried to flag down two white men in a truck to help him as he lay bleeding from his neck wound, but rather than assist him, the two men told him to stay away from their truck, called him a nigger and threatened to kill him. He survived only after being taken to the hospital by an African American couple on whose porch he collapsed after walking back to his neighborhood.

At least eleven men, all black, were shot by whites in the days following the flooding, a fact that no one—including the men who were doing the shooting—seems particularly afraid to acknowledge. Several of the perpetrators admit to seeing black men shot and admit to personally shooting at them. One of the white terrorists, Wayne Janak, brags about keeping the bloody shirt of one victim as a trophy, and cheerfully recollects seeing three black men shot in one day. In a telling comparison, Janak likened the actions of the white gunmen to "pheasant season in South Dakota." As Janak put it, "If it moved you shot it."

A. C. Thompson's investigative report on the terrorist activity of the white thugs included descriptions of racist depravity almost too extreme to fathom:

> Some of the gunmen prowling Algiers Point were
> out to wage a race war, says one woman whose uncle
> and two cousins joined the cause. A former New

Orleanian, this source spoke to me anonymously because she fears her relatives could be prosecuted for their crimes. "My uncle was very excited that it was a free-for-all—white against black—that he could participate in," says the woman. "For him, the opportunity to hunt black people was a joy."

"They didn't want any of the 'ghetto niggers' coming over from the east side of the river," she says, adding that her relatives viewed African Americans who wandered into Algiers Point as "fair game." One of her cousins, a young man in his 20s, sent an e-mail to her and several other family members describing his adventures with the militia. He had attached a photo in which he posed next to an African American man who'd been fatally shot. The tone of the e-mail, she says, was "gleeful"—her cousin was happy that "they were shooting niggers."

An Algiers Point homeowner who wasn't involved in the shootings describes another attack. "All I can tell you is what I saw," says the white resident, who asked to remain anonymous for fear of reprisals. He witnessed a barrage of gunfire—from a shotgun, an AK-47 and a handgun—directed by militiamen at two African-American men standing on Pelican Street, not too far from Janak's place. The gunfire hit one of them. "I saw blood squirting out of his back," he says. "I'm an EMT. My instinct should've been to rush to him. But I didn't. And if I had, those guys"—the militiamen—"might have opened up on me, too."

The witness shows me a home video he record-ed shortly after the storm. On the tape, three white Algiers Point men discuss the incident. One says it might be a bad idea to talk candidly about the crime. Another dismisses the notion, claiming, "No jury would convict."[88]

As predicted by this member of the Algiers Point ter-rorist squad, no one has been punished for these crimes. Indeed, no official investigation by law enforcement has occurred at all.

But beyond evidence such as this, to understand how prevalent racism and white privilege remain in the nation one need look no further than the presidential campaign itself, during which any number of fairly blatant examples managed to manifest.

Racism in the Presidential Campaign

From racist and religiously bigoted e-mails claiming Obama to be a "Muslim terrorist," who wasn't really born in America and who was viciously anti-white, to T-shirts with racist caricatures of the Senator, to video footage of whites spouting racist calumny upon him, evidence of raw and unfiltered Racism 1.0 was ubiquitous. Likewise, white denial about that racism was also in full effect. So, for instance, when the Chaffey County, California, Republican Women's Club sent out a mailer to its members called "Obama Bucks," in which the senator was featured on the front of a food-stamp certificate, surrounded by pictures of fried chicken and watermelon, the president of the club insisted there was nothing racist about the mailing at all. Another member, defending the mailing, explained that "everyone eats those foods," and so the fact that they have long been stereotypically associated with African Americans was a mere coincidence.[89]

Attempts by Obama's opponents and their surrogates to inject race into the campaign and to play upon white racial fears and resentments were also common. Although the far right was especially implicated in such efforts, these thinly veiled racial buttons were first pushed during the primary season, by Senator Hillary Clinton's campaign. So in the spring of 2008, when former congresswoman and vice-presidential candidate Geraldine Ferraro (a key Clinton supporter) remarked that Obama wouldn't be where he was were it not for his race, she was dipping into the well of white racial resentment and racism, whether or not that had been her purpose. It wasn't that Ferraro's remark was racist in the traditional sense, for in that regard it wasn't. There was no apparent bigotry behind it, no implicit assumption, for example, that it would be bad for the United States to have a president of color. Yet—and this is a point that goes to the very heart of the difference between the way that white folks and folks of color understand the concept of racism—Ferraro's intent is not what mattered. What mattered then, and matters now, is that by suggesting Obama's success has been due solely, or at least mostly, to his race, Ferraro directly played into, perpetuated and stoked the flames of one of the dominant narratives about race in the white community: namely, that blacks are getting things they don't deserve and for which they aren't really qualified. It was to suggest, however unintentionally, that Obama was little more than an electoral affirmative action case.

Likewise, when Senator Clinton slapped Obama with the tag of "elitist" for noting that rural folks often cling to guns and religion when times are tight economically—a point that white author Thomas Frank had made in his best-selling book *What's the Matter With Kansas?* in 2005, with very little objection from anyone—she was, whether deliberately or not, feeding into white racial resentment and ultimately, racism itself. To paint a man of color as "elitist" and out-of-touch with average people (and this coming from a Wellesley grad) is to push all the "uppity Negro" buttons that have been among the favorites of white bigots for years. Given the long-standing racial order, in which whites have been able to take for granted that even if they didn't have much "at least they weren't black," to now be confronted with a black man who has more education than they do, and has accomplished more than they have in a professional sense, is to have the "psychological wage of whiteness," as W. E. B. DuBois called it, reduced in real dollar terms. It is to upset the applecart. And to then push the elitist button—in effect, to remind white voters that this black guy is not like you, in fact he looks down on you, and how dare he—is one of the oldest and most predictable plays in the racist playbook. In the past, this kind of invective precipitated white riots against black communities, as with the destruction of the Greenwood district in Tulsa in 1921. Now, it may not lead to such orgiastic displays of violence, and it may not even be sufficient to derail a campaign the likes of Obama's (as it clearly wasn't), but it certainly created additional hurdles for Obama to leap, and could create a latent resentment that could re-emerge in years to come.

As Obama clinched the nomination and the country moved into the height of the general election campaign, things only got worse. Thus, the constant stream of rhetoric from the McCain/Palin camp, aimed at whites, which said, in effect, "We're one of you," and he (meaning Obama) is not. He's the East Coast educated liberal elitist, while we are a ticket made up of a fighter pilot and, don't forget, former POW, and a hockey mom. He's a self-appointed messiah, while we are the arbiters of small-town values. He's the arrogant "cool kid," while we're like your neighbors.

That none of these arguments may seem racial in nature only speaks to how little whites—with no experience being subjugated by another race—understand the underlying psychology of race, and the way that language and symbols take on meaning individually and socially in ways that often go unacknowledged. So the hockey-mom label for Sarah Palin, while seemingly innocent, perfectly primes a white racial frame of "she's one of us," even for those whites who don't play hockey. Hockey couldn't be a whiter sport in the eyes of most, and indeed it's even better for this purpose than soccer, which is played mostly by folks of color the world over. So when you play up a vice-presidential candidate's credentials as a hockey mom (which has no relevance to her fitness to help run a country), what you're saying is, "Vote for these folks because they are like you." That many whites interviewed shortly after the Palin selection remarked upon how they liked her because she's like the mom next door (not that the mom next door has any qualifications to potentially become president) suggests that the frame had a certain salience, and for many was effective in reassuring white voters that the GOP ticket was "looking out for them," while those other guys were dangerous interlopers from whom they needed to be protected.

Similarly, the media framing of Governor Palin as an outdoorsy, gritty, moose-hunting pioneer, while perhaps accurate (if a bit overplayed), was almost certain to trigger any number of racial associations in the minds of white voters: the pioneer narrative (which a white Alaskan conjures almost by their mere existence) is, after all, one in which brave white folks are seen as conquering the wilderness and the unknown by dint of our hard work, determination, and strong values. It is part and parcel of the founding mythos of the United States, and at a time when whites are exhibiting increasing anxiety about demographic change, immigration, and a popular culture that many see as having been virtually hijacked by celebrities of color, it is a mythos that provides comfort, the hopes of a return to normalcy, and a sense of belonging to the dominant group, whose members fear their dominance is slipping.

When *Newsweek* can put a picture of Sarah Palin on its cover holding a rifle, as it did in its September 15, 2008, edition, and millions of white folks can find that image reassuring, we know whiteness is being played to, and deployed, quite effectively. After all, were Michelle Obama to be pictured with a gun, any gun, it is doubtful that white readers would find such an image to be little more than a patriotic hat-tip to the Second Amendment. Black people with guns scare most white folks. White people with guns are the first line of defense against the dangerous "other," and so Sarah Palin and her pugnacious white-guy running mate (who, recall, also knows how to fire a weapon, or at least how to drop bombs from planes) can be viewed as our protectors, and those who will guard us from the outside enemy: the terrorists, the domestic thugs, or the black presidential candidate who's getting a little too big for his britches.

And speaking of thugs, just two weeks before the election, McCain staffers were pushing a story to the media about Ashley Todd, a McCain volunteer from Texas, who allegedly had been mugged by a dark-skinned black man at an ATM machine in Pittsburgh. The man, according to Todd, scrawled a "B" on her cheek (presumably for Barack) after seeing her McCain bumper sticker. That the story turned out to be totally false—and Todd later admitted to having concocted it—didn't alter the fact that the McCain camp had been willing to believe the lie and circulate it to journalists like Jonathan Martin of Politico.com, in a way calculated to play to white fear.[90]

Likewise, radio commentator Rush Limbaugh spent the better part of three days insisting that Colin Powell's endorsement of Barack Obama had been merely an act of racial bonding. Powell, the lifelong Republican and confidant to both Presidents Bush, had chosen to support Obama simply because of a shared skin color, to hear Limbaugh tell it. That Powell could have believed Obama the better candidate was not conceivable to Limbaugh, even as several white Republicans and conservatives also endorsed Obama, such as Christopher Buckley (son of the late William F. Buckley, the godfather of the modern conservative movement); Susan Eisenhower, granddaughter of the late president Dwight D. Eisenhower; neoconservative hawk Kenneth Adelman; and ultra-conservative talk show host Michael Smerconish.[91] That Limbaugh would seek to racialize the Powell endorsement, given the other endorsements by white Republicans and conservatives mentioned here (and there were several others), suggests that he actually knew better, but also felt confident that pushing the button of racial resentment with his mostly white audience would pay dividends, if not on election day, at least down the line. By fostering a siege mentality whereby people of color can be viewed as "ganging up" on white Americans, conservatives like Limbaugh—or others who intimated that Obama's virtually unanimous support in the black community was "reverse racism" rather than the result of blacks identifying with the Democratic Party—can seek to exploit white fears in response to an Obama presidency. Though the pushing of this button failed to pay off for the right in 2008 as it had in prior elections (such as 1988, with the infamous "Willie Horton" ad used against Michael Dukakis), priming the pump of racial resentment could yet create greater racial tension in the future.

Along these same lines, right-wing commentators including Limbaugh, Neil Cavuto of Fox News, columnist Charles Krauthammer, and others spent the latter part of October seeking to pin the blame for the nation's housing and financial crisis on poor folks and people of color, and thereby push racial anger buttons as voters prepared to go to the polls. This they did by suggesting that the responsibility for the mess lay almost entirely with laws like the Community Reinvestment Act (which seeks to steer investments into previously underserved neighborhoods and ensure that credit is available to persons in such communities who can qualify for loans) and groups like ACORN, which work at the grassroots level to open up credit access for lower-income folks in cities across the country. To hear these commentators tell it, had it not been for ACORN "forcing" banks to give loans to people in "bad neighborhoods" who had no business being homeowners, or if it hadn't been for laws like CRA and the civil rights groups who pushed for their implementation, requiring loans to "minorities and other risky folks" as Cavuto put it, the subprime mortgage mess and the full-scale financial collapse it has triggered would never have occurred. To wit, the *Wall Street Journal*'s editorial page on September 27, 2008, which chimed in to suggest, "ACORN has promoted laws like the CRA, which laid the foundation for the house of cards built out of subprime loans."[92]

But in fact, almost nothing the right has said about CRA or ACORN has even a remote resemblance to the truth. To begin with, the Community Reinvestment Act only applies to federally insured depository institutions such as banks and thrifts (like savings and loans). It does not apply at all to independent mortgage brokers, and yet it is these brokers who are responsible for the vast majority of subprime loans. Furthermore, the loans written under the CRA actually perform well, in part because the underwriting standards are fairly stringent and, unlike many of the subprime loans written by mortgage brokers, do require verification of income and ability to repay the loan in question. In fact, loans written by the institutions not covered by CRA have foreclosure rates four to five times higher than those for CRA-covered institutions, suggesting that if anything, CRA engenders responsible lending, rather than its opposite.

So too is ACORN inaccurately blamed. Not only has ACORN not encouraged or forced irresponsible lending to the poor or persons of color, but indeed its mortgage assistance program only helps borrowers get deals if they first go through counseling on budget and credit issues, and if they have a demonstrated capacity to repay the loan taken out. This is likely why loans procured with the assistance of ACORN have a virtually nonexistent foreclosure rate of less than one-third of one percent, making it one of the biggest success stories in housing of the past half century.[93]

By seeking to blame poor folks, people of color, and the groups that advocate for them for the financial troubles of the nation—and especially when combined with their bogus claims that ACORN had engaged in "massive voter fraud" so as to steal the election for Obama—the right may well manage to foster greater racial resentments and backlash against an Obama administration as we move forward.[94] That its efforts to scapegoat such persons as these failed to sink Obama's campaign chances is perhaps reassuring, but the potential for the right to poison the well of race relations with such rhetoric remains quite real.

Indeed, immediately after Obama was elected a spate of overtly racist incidents suggests this backlash, cultivated by the right, may already be in full swing. Within two weeks of Obama's victory, several stories about nooses hung on college campuses, or Obama effigies, or racist and anti-Obama graffiti, or death threats against the president-elect had surfaced. In Pennsylvania, a white teacher's aide was suspended for telling a black student that Obama would be assassinated, that the country would be ruined with him in office, and that he would likely change the American flag to the KFC sign.[95] In one Idaho town, elementary school children on the bus chanted "Assassinate Obama" a week after the election, much to the chagrin of one student who told her parents,[96] and elsewhere, mostly in small towns, whites displeased with the election of Obama made their views known in terms that rarely sought to veil their racial animus.[97]

But in spite of all the racially coded campaign language, and even the blatantly racist appeals of others, one might argue—and I'm confident many will—that since

Obama ultimately won, this is yet more confirmation that entrenched white bigotry, though still present in small pockets, nonetheless is on the way out. Yes, white racism is still out there, but clearly not enough to stop persons of color from advancing and succeeding. Which brings us to the second question so often asked in the months leading up to the election.

WAS WHITE AMERICA READY FOR A BLACK PRESIDENT? THE TRIUMPH OF RACISM 2.0

Given Barack Obama's victory in November 2008, it might be tempting to conclude that the question "Was white America ready for a black president" has been answered, and with a resounding "yes." And yet, a few words of caution are probably wise at this stage. Most importantly, it may be that rather than asking this question, the better question to ask would have been under what circumstances is white America ready for a black president? And what kind of black president are we prepared, collectively, to accept?

THE TROUBLE WITH TRANSCENDENCE

Though it is important to challenge the kind of old-fashioned racism that would prevent a white voter from supporting a candidate of color (and the kind mentioned above that is being manifested since Obama's victory) it is at least as important and perhaps more so that we come to understand the more subtle forms of racism, which may well animate even those whites who are willing to vote for someone like Obama. For while it may be tempting for the press (and most definitely for white Obama supporters) to seek to create a dichotomy whereby the "bad whites" are the ones who voted against the black guy, while the "good whites" are the ones who voted for him, such a dualism is more than a little simplistic, for any number of reasons.

To start, in a campaign where Obama was lauded for "transcending race," or "moving beyond race," knowing how much his white supporters really get the issue of racism, or how much they've checked their own at the door remains an open question. To the extent Obama is seen by many whites as different than most black folks—and make no mistake, this is how very many whites see him, by their own admission—it is quite possible that among his voter base one can find large numbers of whites whose views about the larger black community, or other communities of color, are anything but enlightened.

So consider briefly the implications of comments made by white Obama supporters that were quoted in a front-page article from the November 10, 2007, *Wall Street Journal*, and what they mean in terms of white folks' racial attitudes, even when these whites are willing to vote for a particular black man for president.[98] From one we hear that Obama is his pick because he makes white people "feel good" about ourselves. Though the reason for which this Obama supporter values his candidate as the political equivalent of Zoloft—a popular antidepressant medication—is unclear, venturing an educated guess isn't an especially daunting task. Given the context of the story, and the fact that it is white people in particular who the voter notes are made to feel good by Obama, there are few reasons one can imagine, other than the fact that Obama's avoidance of "too much" race talk is the mechanism by which the palliative is transmitted.

Then comes Bob Tuke, former chair of the Tennessee Democratic Party, who notes with no apparent sense of irony or misgiving that Obama, by virtue of his race-averse approach has "emancipated" whites to finally vote for a black candidate. Emancipated. Yes, as in, freed from bondage. It's as if Tuke, an enthusiastic Obama backer, envisions Obama as a modern-day Lincoln, only this time freeing white folks from the chains of their racist bigotry.

But without question, the most disturbing comment of all came from a young, Nashville-based political blogger who intoned that what he liked about the Illinois Senator is that he "doesn't come with the baggage of the civil rights movement." While you are letting the full implications of that statement sink in, let it suffice to say that when the civil rights movement—which must stand as one of the greatest struggles for human liberation in the history of our collective species—can be equated with Samsonite, with luggage, with something one should avoid as though it were radioactive (and all of this being said by a young white liberal, albeit one who goes on to say that because he has black friends and listens to rap music, this somehow proves his own racial enlightenment), well, we are at a very dangerous place in the history of our nation's evolution, all celebrations of Obama's cross-racial appeal notwithstanding.

If large numbers of white folks embraced Obama, but only because of his ability to "transcend race," by which we really mean transcend his own blackness, doesn't this suggest the ongoing power of whiteness and racist thinking? And isn't the entire concept of "transcending blackness" in and of itself racist, insofar as it presumes, if only by implication, that there is something negative about blackness— something to be avoided, or if it can't be avoided, at least finessed, worked around, or smoothed over? To praise the transcending of blackness, after all, is to imply that blackness is something negative, something from which one who might otherwise qualify for membership ought to seek escape, and quickly. It's the political equivalent of a white person telling their black friend or colleague, "I don't even think of you as black," and not understanding why the friend or colleague is offended, not recognizing that the subtle subtext of such a statement is that it's a good thing the white person doesn't think of them as black, because if they did, the black person so thought of would be up the proverbial creek without the proverbial paddle. And of course, to the extent no white politician is ever asked to transcend his or hers race (i.e., whiteness), that racial transcendence is experienced as an unequal burden seems beyond dispute.

What we are left with is the almost unavoidable conclusion that Obama has become the Cliff Huxtable of politics: a black man with whom millions of whites can identify and to whom they can relate, as with the former TV dad from *The Cosby Show*. On the one hand, this proved beneficial to him as a candidate, and to the extent it allows certain white stereotypes of black men to be challenged, perhaps it could also be positive for the nation as a whole. But on the other hand, if Obama sets a standard that white folks then come to need in all other black men—if we use the Obama model as an archetype, or a template for acceptable, respectable black males generally, such that anyone who doesn't as effortlessly transcend their blackness (or who merely doesn't want to) is shunned—then all we will have accomplished on the racial front is the reinforcing of anti-black antipathy. If, in order to be acceptable to whites, folks of color have to speak a certain way, look a certain way, evince a certain level of erudition, have been educated at the nation's finest institutions, avoid discussing race and racism, and generally make us comfortable with their existence—in other words, if we are only willing to accept them on our terms—then racism has not been trumped so much as it has merely taken on a new and more subtle form.

And this is what I fear has been missed, even by many of the white folks who are enthusiastic about Obama. Because we are so used to thinking of racism as the traditional rejectionism and blatant bigotry of the past, we sometimes miss the subtle ways in which racism has shape-shifted to fit more comfortably within a modern context. But if whites are able to view Obama positively only because we don't see him the way we see most black folks, then the implication is that black folks are generally still seen quite negatively by the white masses. In which case, we are dealing with that Racism 2.0, or enlightened exceptionalism, which allows whites to carve out exceptions—perhaps even large ones—for certain folks, but continue to both harbor substantial racial biases towards most persons of color and deny equal access and privilege to the black and brown community. In this sense, racism has become something like those balloons that clowns blow up at children's birthday parties, the ones that change shape from a dog to a bunny rabbit when you squeeze the air from one end to the next. But let us remember that despite the shape-shifting, at the end of the day, what we are left with is still a balloon. And so too with racism, whether of the 1.0 or 2.0 variety.

REINFORCING THE DOMINANT NARRATIVE

Among the central needs of white voters when it came to relating to Obama—and it was among the things that no doubt assisted him most in convincing so many whites to support him—was his warm embrace of the dominant national narrative generally accepted by the white majority. By endorsing a vision of the nation commonly believed by whites, Obama could in effect distance himself from the larger black community, which has long seen the United States far differently than most white Americans have, due to the way in which they have experienced its institutions. For persons in the throes of Racism 2.0, such distancing would be central to their ability to carve out an exception for someone like Obama, precisely because they would be more likely to accept him as a non-threatening man of color. And indeed Obama did everything he could to be non-threatening. Beginning with his first national speech, at the 2004 Democratic National Convention—which served as his first true introduction to the nation—Obama praised America as a "magical place" and a place of "freedom and opportunity," in which the needs of whites and persons of color weren't really all that different: a theme he would repeat often in *The Audacity of Hope* as well.[99] And whereas black leaders in the past had always sought to challenge the institutions of their nation, even as they appealed to the best in the American tradition, Obama rarely if at all critiques the fundamental structures of American society. Indeed, he seems to go out of his way to praise them, something that no doubt is soothing to white folks.

In his race speech (a speech which, however poignant and powerful it was, he would never have given had he not been forced to by the circumstances surrounding reaction to Rev. Jeremiah Wright), Obama played to white conceptions of the nation's founding, by noting that the founders "traveled across an ocean to escape tyranny and persecution." This is the dominant, which is to say, white version of why they came, one that conveniently forgets the way they behaved once they actually got here, which was to immediately suppress those who didn't worship as they did, to impose the very autocratic cruelties upon others that they felt had been imposed upon them in the motherland, and of course, to tyrannize, unto death, the bulk of the land's native populations.

For much of his race talk Obama criticized Rev. Wright, not merely for his tone but for his understanding of the nation itself, thereby setting up a clear dichotomy for voters, between the "angry black" version of what America has been and is today, and the "kinder, gentler" version he was trying to forward (and which whites, in the main, wholeheartedly accept). And so he blasted Wright for "denigrating both the greatness and goodness of our nation," merely because Wright pointed out the documented crimes of the nation he once served in uniform. Then he essentially placed the blame for racial division in the United States on Wright and others like him, who, according to Obama, fail to appreciate how much the country has changed.

Throughout the speech, whenever Obama did seek to honor the righteous anger still felt by many, even most people of color, regarding racism, he was careful to balance that sympathetic commentary with an equivalent sympathy towards the white perspective. So he mentioned, within the same paragraph, black anger over racism with white anger over affirmative action—as if these two were even remotely equivalent in terms of their legitimacy; as if the very real injury done to black folks for hundreds of years was no greater than the perceived injury to whites from such programs. Even though, according to all the available evidence, these efforts have managed not to alter, by one iota, the economic dominance of whites in America. Interestingly, one could even read his comments as doing more than equating black and white anger; in some respects he was even more doting on white fears and insecurities. Hence his comments in the speech, directed at blacks, that black anger "all too often distracts us from solving real problems ... (and) keeps us from squarely facing our own complicity in our condition." These remarks were nowhere balanced by the notion that white fears too, and white anger too, might be just as unproductive or misdirected. And while he then spent a few seconds directly challenging perceived irresponsibility in the black community and calling for better parenting in black families, he didn't see the need to challenge white parents for passing along in many cases, the vicious pathogen of racism to their kids. Like so many others, Bill Cosby first and foremost, Obama's calls for personal responsibility were almost entirely one-sided, thereby allowing whites to feel a kinship with him and his approach to these matters, and ensuring that only the most reactionary white voter would think him a radical on race issues.

Whether or not one blames Obama for his approach here is not the point. Perhaps one could argue that as a politician, needing white votes, he had little choice. That may well be the case. But we must at least recognize what his need to pander to the perceived needs of the national white electorate means about race and racism in this country. It means this, nothing more and nothing less: White folks are still calling the shots. White folks still hold the power. White folks still get to call the tune. White needs, perspectives, views, and privilege still dominate, and until that changes, profound social injustices against people of color will continue to be perpetuated. The fact that there are some folks of color who can play the tune, and quite well at that, hardly alters the dynamic between those who call it and those who are forced to do the dance. And the danger here is that if we are not extraordinarily careful, Obama's success on white terms may only reinforce the negative feelings that so many whites have about the larger black community, and other communities of color, whose members, on the whole, do not choose to play the game in the same way, or even if they try, fail to live up to the standard set by Obama thus far.

WHITE PERCEPTIONS OF NON-OBAMA-LIKE PEOPLE OF COLOR

That white folks view blacks, by and large, in terms quite different from the way so many of them view Obama is really not debatable, and is strongly confirmed by the results of opinion surveys for the past twenty years, which suggest that most whites hold any number of negative, prejudiced, and ultimately racist beliefs about black people.

Results on opinion surveys vary depending on the way pollsters construct the questions asked, but as a general rule, one thing has been consistent across each of the survey instruments: namely, somewhere in the neighborhood of 60 percent of all whites admit to holding racist views about African Americans. According to a National Opinion Research Center survey in the early 1990s, over 60 percent of whites said they believed that blacks are generally lazier than other groups, 56 percent say that blacks are generally more prone to violence, and over half say that blacks are generally less intelligent than other groups.[100] A similar survey from 1993 found that three in four whites accept as true at least one racist stereotype about African Americans, regarding such items as general laziness, propensity to criminality and violence, intelligence, or work ethic. And according to a 2001 survey, 60 percent of whites, approximately, admit that they believe at least one negative and racist stereotype of blacks: for example, that they are generally lazy, generally aggressive or violent, or prefer to live on welfare rather than work for a living.[101] In fact, the belief in black preference for welfare over work is typically the most commonly believed of the stereotypes; this despite the fact that only a very small percentage of African Americans—and for that matter, a minority of even poor African Americans—receive public assistance.

One other way pollsters manage to demonstrate the racism of whites is to ask questions probing why they believe African Americans, on average, are doing so much worse than whites, in terms of income, education, or poverty rates. In these surveys, subjects are asked to choose from among several factors contributing to racial inequity. These include racism and discrimination by whites against blacks (either past or present), inherent inferiority on the part of blacks, and black characterological or behavioral flaws. In most cases, small numbers say they agree with the notion of inherent black inferiority, somewhat larger numbers blame racism, but the vast majority choose the "character flaw" option, which often amounts to a belief that blacks "lack the appropriate work ethic" to better their lives, or "just don't want to try hard enough," or lack the necessary motivation or values in some way Two-thirds of whites in one survey said the disadvantages suffered by blacks are due to their dependence on welfare, which, again, is an odd claim, seeing as how five out of six blacks don't receive any.[102]

Of course, the irony of these "explanations" for black disadvantage couldn't be much clearer. By claiming that most blacks are morally and behaviorally defective (and doing so as an alternative explanation contrasted with the racism and discrimination option), these whites have embraced an argument that is by definition racist in that it treats millions of African Americans as a mass of pathology, casting a judgment upon them as a group that further stigmatizes them in the eyes of the larger society. If whites said they believed black genes were defective, that they were biologically predisposed to failure, we would immediately recognize such an argument as racist. That whites are now content to settle for explanations that focus on black character defects should hardly strike us as any less so. There is still, even in this claim, a sense of presumed inferiority and superiority, with blacks on the bottom and whites on top.

Other research has found that when whites are shown

pictures of black faces, even for only thirty milliseconds, the parts of their brains that respond to perceived threats light up almost instantaneously,[103] suggesting the connection between blackness and danger that continues to animate much white consciousness. That whites view blacks as dangerous, deviant, and criminal likely helps explain why it was so easy for whites, as mentioned previously, to believe the ultimately false stories coming out of New Orleans in the wake of Katrina concerning rapes, murders, and child molestation in the evacuation centers.

White bias toward average, everyday African Americans also helps explain the findings of a recent study from the University of Illinois–Chicago to the effect that whites rate neighborhoods as lower in quality and desirability based solely on the race of the area's residents, even when other factors such as class status and demeanor are indistinguishable. In the study in question, researchers surveyed over 600 randomly selected whites in the Chicago and Detroit metropolitan areas. They showed the participants video clips of neighborhoods, in which actors posed as residents. The actors engaged in the same activities in each clip, and were paired in each sample, so as to portray similar class statuses and backgrounds, leaving racial identity of the actors/residents as the only variable remaining. Some study participants were shown clips with only white actors/residents, others were shown clips with black residents, and some were shown clips with a mix of black and white actors/residents. The participants were then asked to evaluate the communities on a number of factors, including safety, future likely property values, and the quality of the neighborhood schools. Whites who saw videos with white residents rated neighborhoods far more positively than whites who saw videos with black residents in the identical neighborhood, while whites shown a mixed community rated such neighborhoods in between in terms of desirability.[104]

In keeping with the notion that whites can often accept individual blacks—Obama, Oprah or others—while still holding onto hostile views of blacks generally, consider the implications of research by sociologists Joe Feagin and Leslie Picca in their book *Two-Faced Racism: Whites in the Backstage and Frontstage*. Feagin and Picca had 626 college students keep journals, at schools around the country, in which they recorded any and all incidents, comments or other actions that they personally witnessed, involving some kind of racial issue. In a fairly typical account from one of the journals, one white college student offered telling details about what goes on when he gets together with a certain group of his white male friends:

> When any two of us are together, no racial comments or jokes are ever made. However, with the full group membership present, anti-Semitic jokes abound, as do racial slurs and vastly derogatory

statements. . . . A member of the group . . . decided that he has the perfect idea for a Hallmark card. On the cover it would have a few kittens in a basket with ribbons and lace. On the inside it would simply say, "You're a nigger."[105]

According to Feagin and Picca, they received roughly 9,000 accounts of racial events, with 7,500 of these involving blatantly racist comments, jokes, or performances by whites around their white friends and colleagues. That many of these racist comments and actions came from whites who likely socialize with persons of color, even have "friends" of color, celebrate black entertainers and athletes, and certainly wouldn't consider themselves racist, only further suggests the way that racism often remains hidden behind a veneer of tolerance.

So while we can take some comfort in the way much of white America has embraced Barack Obama, and the way in which millions ultimately voted for him when given a chance to do so, we should exercise great caution in drawing broad and grand conclusions about white racism generally. That many whites view Obama as different, as non-threatening, as acceptable, nonetheless presupposes that those same whites continue to hold onto a range of negative beliefs about the larger black community. And so we have the evidence from the September 2008 AP survey, in which 60 percent of the white Democrats who admitted to holding negative views about black folks in general nonetheless said that they planned to vote for Obama.[106]

While not wanting to overstate it, we might now revisit the previously conjured Cliff Huxtable analogy, for it applies in more ways than might be readily apparent, and the extent to which it does also points to the potential trouble posed by this fact. When *The Cosby Show* introduced the nation to the Huxtable family in the 1980s, it quickly became one of those rare programs to gain the loyalty of both white and black viewers. In its presentation of an upwardly mobile, professional black family (one parent a doctor, the other an attorney), *The Cosby Show* differed in many ways from earlier sitcoms featuring African American characters. A decade earlier, viewers may have watched *Good Times*, which revolved around a working-class family living in Chicago public housing; or *Sanford & Son*, whose principal characters worked in a junkyard in Los Angeles; or *The Jeffersons*, whose story line concerned a nouveau-successful if not entirely rich couple, and whose principal character, George Jefferson, ran a dry cleaning business on the upper east side of New York City. In each case, the black characters were both economically marginalized (or in the case of the Jeffersons, only newly monied, and somewhat out of place in their new digs) and far more stereotypical in their lexicon, demeanor, speech style, and mannerisms. Although these shows, contrary to common critiques, actually went far to humanize their subjects (especially *Good Times*, whose Evans family forged a hard-working, stable, and loving home that in many ways could be read as counter to white stereotypes about folks living in so-called ghettos), because the characters were placed in more typical settings and roles, whites never fully took to them, and often had difficulty relating to their struggles.

Perhaps even more importantly, because these earlier shows often dealt with racial themes (and quite effectively it should be noted), they took a risk of alienating white audiences, who by the 1970s were already tiring of race talk, having come through a decade where such talk had been at the top of the national agenda. *The Cosby Show* deviated from the prior formula in multiple ways: by portraying a highly educated and successful upper-middle-class family, by having that family be identifiably black (Cosby's character, for example, was often seen wearing sweatshirts from historically black colleges, and the Huxtable home featured African art and listened to a lot of Charlie Parker) but yet not too black in the way whites were used to thinking of African American folks: as uneducated, dysfunctional and lower-class. Critically, race as a subject was never part of the Huxtables' life, much as it had never been a part of Cosby's comedy routines.[107] The Huxtable family's challenges were little different from those faced by any other American family, irrespective of color. Their kids talked back and engaged in fairly boilerplate teen hijinks;

they occasionally bickered, after which point they would make up, but never was there any indication that as a black family they confronted specifically race-based obstacles or concerns. That such a rendering would be an absurdist fantasy in the Reagan-Bush 1980s and early 1990s should be obvious, but it nonetheless proved certainly reassuring to white viewers.

And so it won't come as a particular shock to learn that when researchers from the University of Massachusetts convened focus groups of white Cosby viewers, they routinely, and with only a few exceptions, sang the praises of the program. White viewers regularly remarked upon how "normal" the Huxtables seemed, how their challenges as a family were so similar to those of their own families, and how they identified mightily with the Huxtable clan. They were often especially quick to draw a contrast between The Cosby Show and those earlier black-themed programs, usually holding the latter up to scorn while praising the former. As one focus group member explained, *The Cosby Show* "wasn't like a jive show, like *Good Times*. . . . Cosby is more of American down the line. . . ."[108]

A few things should be said about this statement in particular, in that it has considerable relevance for the 2008 presidential race and the way in which whites view Obama. To say that Cosby's character is more "American down the line" than the characters in *Good Times* is to equate, however implicitly, American with white, or, if not white, at least a person of color whose life is a lot like that of a white person. Such a statement is quite revealing, in that it demonstrates a tendency for some among whites to view blacks who don't fit the Huxtable model as less than fully American. It's as if poor or middle-class blacks who don't speak in the dominant linguistic form of standard English have less claim on citizenship than the rest of us. The relevance of this kind of attitude to Obama's candidacy and the future of race relations in the United States should be readily apparent. While Obama may have succeeded in fitting himself within the Huxtable mold in the eyes of white America—or, whether or not he sought it, may now have been fit into that slot by others—the end result could well be the reinforcement of negative views toward those blacks who fail to attain the lofty pinnacle of "Huxtability" achieved by the new president.

This trade-off, whereby certain "acceptable" black folks are admired by whites, even as the larger black community is viewed negatively, did indeed manifest in the case of *The Cosby Show*, much as could happen in the wake of Obama's presidency. According to Sut Jhally and Justin Lewis in their 1992 book, *Enlightened Racism*, whites discussing Cosby often made comments suggesting "if the Huxtables can make it, anyone can." Thus, for the mass of black humanity whom they had come to fear and loathe, that fear and loathing would only be reinforced, multifold, given a glimpse into the way black folks could be, if only they'd put forth the effort to better themselves.

As the authors explained, "The acceptance of the Huxtables as an everyfamily did not dislodge the generally negative associations white viewers have of 'black culture . . .' [T]he price it pays for acceptance is that the Huxtables do appear 'just like white people.'" And by showcasing a successful black family, they note, "*The Cosby Show* provides its white audience with relief not only from fear but also from responsibility."[109] Much in the same way, by dint of his personal success narrative, his life story, and his studious finessing of race issues during his campaign, Obama managed to relieve whites of some of their anti-black anxieties, and certainly release them from worrying too much about black and brown folks, or their issues. Once relieved and mollified, whites were then free to support him in numbers they would never have delivered had he taken a different tack. While this paid substantial personal dividends for Obama, it remains to be seen whether it will merely create new obstacles, new barriers, and new hurdles for average, everyday black folks. If whites embrace Obama but then come to view non-Obama-like black folks even more negatively than before, little will have been accomplished on the racial front in a concrete sense, even as a black man commands the highest position of U.S. and, arguably, global politics.

Indeed, in the wake of Obama's victory, on election night, this precise comparison with Bill Cosby and his acceptable blackness was made, though without the recognition of its problematic nature, by none other than Karl Rove, who explained on Fox News that America had had a black first family before, referring to the Huxtables! Speaking of the fictional family, Rove noted, "It wasn't a black family. It was an American family," at once suggesting that that which is black is not really American, and contributing to the notion that the Huxtables, as with the Obamas, now, transcend their problematic blackness, to the benefit of the nation.[110] But in such a formulation, blackness remains very much a problem to be overcome, and as such, racism—even if it is of the 2.0 variety—remains in evidence.

RACISM 2.0 AND THE DANGEROUS MYTH OF MERITOCRACY

In the days following the election of Barack Obama to the office of the presidency, it was common to hear black folks on television, radio, or in personal conversations saying how because of his victory, they now felt they could look at their children, tell them that they could "be anything they wanted to be," and, for the first time, really mean it. That such a meaningful feeling for millions is touching cannot be denied. For those of us who are white, it may even be jarring to realize that for hundreds of years black parents have been unable to believe in this fundamental message of America, seeing as how it is one that most of us have taken for granted for just as long as folks of color have doubted it. And yet, because Obama's rise to prominence does seem to be a textbook confirmation of the meritocratic notion that is at the heart of the American narrative—the idea that if you work hard and apply yourself you can be anything you want to be—it may pose yet another challenge to the struggle against racism.

Since Racism 2.0 relies principally on characterological judgments about persons of color—they don't work hard enough, for example—the belief in meritocracy is central to its perpetuation. Whereas old-school rejectionism never really fit too well within the meritocratic frame, seeing as how it often rested on the notion that certain people were just superior and others inferior (and so hard work really wasn't enough for some people to succeed), enlightened exceptionalism is almost entirely bound up with notions of individual initiative. In that regard, 150 years after the Dred Scott decision, in which the Supreme Court averred that blacks had no rights that whites were bound to respect, Racism 2.0 has become the quintessential form of racism in the United States.

That Racism 2.0 so neatly dovetails with the myth of meritocracy will make it especially difficult to confront, first because it fits so cozily within the dominant national narrative, and secondly, because in seeming so downright principled (and less blatantly racist than the old-fashioned racism, which holds that persons of color are biologically and genetically inferior to persons of European descent), those who adhere to such racism are far more able to content themselves with the notion that they are not racists at all. By believing that black folks and other folks of color could do better (if only they would try harder), whites hold out the possibility for black and brown advancement, which is something that, historically, white supremacists would refuse to do. What's more, the practitioner of Racism 2.0 can even position themselves as caring, concerned, and beneficent individuals who only want the best for folks of color, and who might even be willing to tutor them, help them, or provide some charitable assistance to their communities, so as to help them "help themselves." These are folks who will see in Obama the ultimate confirmation of their nation's goodness and greatness, the ultimate proof that the sky is the limit and that barriers of race are no match for the determined will, despite all the aforementioned evidence suggesting that it is, shall we say, just a tad bit more complicated than that.

But by reinforcing the perception of meritocracy as more than just a nice theory—by allowing folks to see it even more than ever as a descriptive truth—Obama's success could (again, if we are not extraordinarily careful) make the fight against racism more difficult than ever, seeing as how meritocracy may be the cornerstone of modern racism itself. If we are taught—and we are, most all of us, irrespective of race or economic status—that anyone can make it if they try hard enough, then isn't it to be expected that those who haven't "made it" will come to be viewed as especially damaged, and as the source of their own sorry station in life? And if folks can then look around and see that among those who haven't "made it" are a disproportionate number of persons of color, doesn't it become almost logical (albeit horribly wrongheaded) to conclude that there must be something wrong with black and brown folks? Doesn't it become easier to rationalize racial domination and inequity, to rationalize white advantage and privilege, and to accept blatant injustices on a mass scale, since they can be written off to aggregate gaps in effort, ambition, or work ethic between whites on the one hand and blacks and Latinos on the other?

RACISM 2.0 AND THE PROBLEM OF STEREOTYPE THREAT

And there is one final consideration here as well: namely, that Obama's success on white terms—and the emergence of Racism 2.0, which would create massive pressure on blacks to live up to the standard set by Obama and disprove the hostile stereotypes still held by millions—could result in the intensification of what Claude Steele (the chair of the psychology department at Stanford) and his colleagues refer to as "stereotype threat" or stereotype vulnerability. According to Steele's research, when persons are members of groups that face common and well-known stigmas or stereotypes and are then placed in a situation where their performance is subject to an evaluation that could result in their being viewed through the lens of the group stereotype—such as black students taking tests, confronted by the fear that if they do poorly, their performance might be seen as evidence of a group intelligence deficit—the anxiety generated is so intense as to often drive down performance, even when one is highly capable of performing the task in question. So when black students have been given experimental standardized tests, for instance, before which they are told that the test they are taking is truly diagnostic of their abilities, they routinely underperform white test-takers, even as similarly qualified blacks, given the same test and told that it says nothing about actual ability, demonstrate no essential difference with white test-takers. Confirmed over and again—and not only with blacks relative to whites, but also women relative to men on math exams, whites relative to Asians on math tests, and whites relative to blacks in athletic competition—this research suggests that when individuals fear living down to a common group stereotype, they will often perform worse than their actual abilities would predict. Likewise, when such fears are removed—by telling test-takers the tests are non-diagnostic, for instance—performance is more equitable. This would indicate that performance gaps in the real world likely tell us quite a bit less about true ability than we've been led to believe, and quite a bit more about performance anxieties created by systemic racism and the awareness of it on the part of its targets.[111]

Given that Obama's success runs the risk of generating expectations about (and a standard for) acceptable black-ness, so to speak, those concerned about stereotype threat should recognize the dangers here: namely, it is quite pos-sible that highly capable students of color, worried about overcoming group stereotypes—and confirming their Obama-like qualities in the eyes of white teachers, bosses, and others—may experience such additional anxiety due to the pressures to live up to this lofty pinnacle, that their performance actually suffers. If so, this underperformance would then serve to "justify," in the eyes of many whites, denying them additional opportunities, from admission to selective schools to certain jobs and promotions.

The bottom line, and this is the lesson to take away from the 2008 campaign: irrespective of Obama's victory, historical racism and the heinous legacy of centuries of slavery and white domination, will remain an issue for the nation to address, as it has been for the last several hun-dred years. And to the extent Obama's political ascent may reinforce white denial, both about ongoing institutional-ized inequities and about white prejudices on a personal level, it may become one of those issues that becomes ever harder to address. The meaning of Obama remains to be seen, but we can and must expect those with an interest in papering over racism and changing the subject to use him for precisely those purposes. If we allow them to suc-ceed in this, his success, however far it goes, will stand as a horrible setback on the road to liberation from racial and social injustice and inequity. If, on the other hand, we say no—if we say that we will not allow this one man's rise to serve as a stand-in for the experiences of the nearly 100 million people of color in this country, people whose lives and degree of acceptance by white folks are quite differ-ent from Obama's—then we may yet be able to mobilize those millions energized by his efforts and his campaign into longer-term work on the road to true freedom and equity. We may, in that case be able to experience Obama, symbolically, as adrenaline, rather than anesthesia.

But that will be, as it has always been, up to all of us: peoples of color and whites, united in purpose and commit-ment to, as James Baldwin put it, "achieving our country."

TWO

The Audacity of Truth: A Call for White Responsibility

Several months ago, I had the occasion to appear jointly at a function in York, Pennsylvania, with my good friend and fellow antiracist educator, Eddie Moore Jr., founder of the nationally renowned White Privilege Conference. Eddie and I were sitting in the offices of the York County Community Against Racism, discussing the presidential campaign with members of the group, wondering about how much of a role race would play in the outcome and generally theorizing and speculating as folks often do in the midst of a hot election season. Every time someone would express confidence in Obama's chances, Eddie would smile a bit, shake his head slowly, aim his visage downward and repeat the same words: "I'm just saying, you better have a backup plan."

Unsure as to what he meant, a few of the gathered locals asked him to clarify—something he was only too glad to do.

"All I'm saying is, I haven't seen whiteness lose yet. So you'd better have a backup plan."

In other words, for persons who were actively engaged in the fight against racism, hope is not audacious (in Obama's terms) so much as it is dangerous. Taken to an extreme, hope can cause us to forfeit our agency, to become so dependent on the outcome of a certain event like an election, that if things turn out differently than we'd hoped for, the resulting deflation can be nearly catastrophic. Eddie was merely saying be prepared, and don't hang your hopes too much on an Obama victory. As a black man in America, he had yet to see whiteness defeated, and frankly, wasn't expecting this time to be much different.

I joked with Eddie a bit, asking him if perhaps whiteness might, in this instance, be somewhat like the New England Patriots heading into the Super Bowl that previous January. There they were, entering the contest undefeated and heavily favored to win as they had always done before, all season long, only to be felled in the end by the New York Giants, a team that had already lost six previous times that year.

Eddie laughed a bit, appreciating the analogy, and then repeated his mantra once again: I'm just saying, have a backup plan. And as he would tell me several months later, indeed, as I was putting the finishing touches on this volume: "All I know is, when folks are hurting, losing their homes, can't afford health care, stuck in a war they can't get out of, I've never seen them turn to a brother, even once—that's all I'm saying." Though he expressed the sentiment with his characteristic smile, what the smile hid—as did my laughter in response to his statement—was a deep and abiding sense of sadness, or so it seemed. Sadness that this truth he was speaking signaled the presence of a lingering sickness, the existence of which the infected were still trying to deny, to downplay, against all the evidence of its metastasis.

Of course, as we now know, Eddie's pessimism about Obama's chances was, although understandable, ultimately unjustified. But thinking about his comment—the one about needing the backup plan—I have come to realize something: namely, even with Barack Obama as the forty-fourth president of the United States, we will still need a back-up plan. For Obama cannot be relied upon, any more so than any other president or national leader, to shepherd our nation out of the wilderness of racism and inequality. The job is too great, and the single solitary man too small for such an effort. Which is to say that if we want the job done right, we're going to have to do it ourselves, all of us.

The worst possible outcome of the 2008 election would be for Obama to have won, only to then have the millions of people mobilized by his mantra of change go back to sleep, to hit the snooze button on the none-too-subtle alarm clock that has been going off for many a year now, and which signals the crisis at hand. If the throngs who flocked to his speeches, and sent him hard-earned money they barely had to give, and went door-to-door canvassing for his campaign, and voted perhaps for the first time, decide that an Obama presidency will serve as a curative for the nation's racial ailment, then all the excitement, all the hope, and all the paeans to "Change" will be for naught. This job was never his to tackle, it was ours. In that sense, we might remind ourselves that Obama cut his teeth as a community organizer, and that the role of the community organizer is not to swoop in and solve the people's problems: rather, it is to help the people see their own strength, their own wisdom, so that they may, themselves, stand up to and fight back against the injustices imposed on them.

Nothing could be more dangerous than for us to fall prey to the irrational exuberance that often characterized public reaction to the Obama campaign. While there were many reasons to be excited about his candidacy, statements by persons like Oprah Winfrey to the effect that Obama was the "fulfillment of Dr. King's dream," or something along those lines, couldn't be more absurd. To hear Winfrey and many others tell it, Dr. King's dream was merely one in which individuals would be judged "on the content of their character" rather than on the basis of skin color, and thus be able to rise to the ranks of the presidency, or, in her case, build an entertainment empire of dizzying proportions. But King's dream was never this individualistic or limited in scope. To suggest such a puny vision on his part is to capitulate to the safe, marketable image of King peddled for at least two decades by those who can't afford the radical Dr. King to be spoken of, let alone celebrated: the King who called the United States the "greatest purveyor of violence in the world today," who came to conclude that traditional capitalism is an inherently destructive system inconsistent with democracy and who called for hundreds of billions in reparations, not only for the black and brown victims of racial injustice, but for the poor of all colors, immiserated by an economics of exploitation. That part of King's dream was never mentioned by candidate Obama, and as such, will not likely be fulfilled by him.

So whether it be to Winfrey or to those persons selling Obama T-shirts that had a picture of King, side-by-side with the candidate, reading, "His Dream, Our Reality," caution is the best advice I can offer. Let us not get carried away, for the moment is too vital, too precious to be left to chance, too critical to engage in an act of mere wish fulfillment, absent a concrete understanding of what will be needed to move that act from the wish column into the column of dreams recognized. There is work to be done if we are to turn the energy of the past year or so into something productive, something that can move us further down the road to social justice.

What is to be done?

Whites must take personal responsibility for addressing racism and white privilege. To begin with, we need to be clear that this problem—this race problem as the pundits have long called it—is a white problem. Make no mistake, it is a problem for people of color, but it is a problem of white folks, by which I mean, racism today is a direct descendant of centuries of slavery and indigenous slaughter perpetuated by whites; white people enacted and enforced violent racist laws and social codes, and though those laws have been repealed one by one since the passage of the Thirteenth Amendment in 1865, the social consciousness, domination, and exclusion of people of color has been passed down since then and remains with us today. Indeed, it was the process of exclusion and subordination that made necessary the lie of black inferiority: after all, to accept that all men and women were truly equal, while still mightily oppressing large segments of that same national population on the basis of skin color, would be to lay bare the falsity of the American creed. And so, to the extent we still live with racist ideology and beliefs, we are still grappling with that white-created thought system and

institutional structure. Whites have sustained racial oppression for generations, either by direct actions aimed at
this purpose, or by silence and complicity, but either way
with the same abominable result. Unless and until those
of us called white take personal responsibility (a term we
love in this culture, but only when aimed like a dagger at
people of color in an attempt to get them to shape up) and
join with leadership of color to undo systems of racism
and white racial privilege, it is a very open question as to
when, or if, the gears of the system of white supremacy
and racism will ever stop turning. And this I say not to
diminish the power and leadership of the black freedom
struggle—the centuries-old movement to abolish all forms
of racial domination—but merely to suggest that achieving greater levels of participatory democracy rooted in social justice in the United States requires work on all sides
of the color line.

So just as Barack Obama saw fit to lecture black men,
and pretty much only black men, on Father's Day in 2008,
admonishing them to do better, to be more responsible, to
support their children and the mothers of their children,
to work hard, to stay sober, to be men in the most positive
sense of the word, so too must whites be reminded of our
personal responsibility. For the concept of responsibility
is, if it is to have any constructive meaning whatsoever,
a two-way or even multidirectional street. If black and
brown peoples must be expected to do better—and there

is nothing wrong with that notion, even if it stems from many an overdrawn and overwrought stereotype suggesting their collective pathology—then so too must white folks do better. If black and brown folks are to be expected to try hard, to put forth maximum effort, to soldier on no matter the existence of institutional racism, so be it. But then so too must white folks put forth maximum effort to eradicate the oppression, exclusion, violence, and discrimination that plagues others, irrespective of how we think others are behaving. For whites to shirk responsibility—and after all, it is only whites who can take responsibility for our prejudices, our discriminatory actions, or the privileges that we receive, either actively or passively—is to use the notion of personal responsibility not as a tool for liberation but as a bludgeon.

So we must take seriously the charge given us by those black activists who have historically led and continue to lead the fight against both formal and informal apartheid in this country. And that charge has long been that we should go back into our communities and talk to white people in a way that they, as people of color, could not. For while we may lament the fact that whites, even at this late date, will usually not listen to a person of color laying out the truth of our nation's racial disparities, we cannot run from that fact, or allow our lamentations over this distressing reality to somehow take the place of action intended to correct it. And so if whites will not listen to voices from black and brown communities, then fine, they will have to hear it from their own. And not just once, but over and again, until they are so tired of hearing it from us that they will either change their thinking, or get the hell out of the way. Perhaps, just maybe, they will even begin to hear it from people of color, once they realize that their own sons and daughters and nephews and nieces are saying the same thing.

Confronting racism is white folks' responsibility because even though we, in the present, are not to blame for the system we have inherited, the fact is, we have inherited it nonetheless, and continue to benefit, consciously or not, from the entrenched privileges that are the legacy of that system. Centuries of black- and brown-led organizing and leadership have resulted in years of steady advances, but the historical inertia remains. Though we learned, perhaps in fifth grade science class, about this concept of inertia—the notion that an object will continue in its existing state of rest or uniform motion in a straight line, unless that state is changed by an external force—what our teachers in all likelihood failed to express (and not for lack of knowing it so much as for the fear of admitting it), was that inertia is not, in the end, a mere property of the physical universe. It is more than that. It is a property of the socioeconomic, the cultural, and the political universe as well. That which happens in one generation affects the next, and so on, and in the very same way as before, until and unless something, some force, produces a change. If we are going to publicly educate our children about the positives of U.S. history, then so too must we be honest and forthright about the negatives. If we are to make use of the assets (as we really cannot help but do) accumulated over a period of several hundred years—including, of course, assets whose possession owes directly and indirectly to slavery and its legacy of racial subordination that enriched many and brutally oppressed many more—then we cannot, ethically, turn our backs on the debts accumulated at the same time.

Whites must learn to listen to (and believe) what people of color say about racism, especially in their own lives. Beyond taking up racism and the struggle against it as both a personal and national responsibility, we must additionally come to appreciate that part of taking responsibility—and maybe one of the biggest parts—is learning to listen, and not merely to listen but to believe what people of color tell us about their own lives. And not just those persons of color who reassure us of how wonderful our nation is, or who make us feel good, as is the case, apparently, with Obama, but black and brown folks who have no desire to soft-pedal the truth for whatever purposes, personal or political. For generations this has been among the greatest stumbling blocks for white Americans. We fail to believe that the pain is real, the anger substantiated, that the experiences about which most every person of color can tell us in great detail, are genuine. Rather, we insist that those who point out racism, in either their own lives or the life of the nation, are exaggerating, playing the race card, or making excuses for their own inadequacies.

Indeed, for anyone to deny the racism that people of color experience, is itself a racist act, in that it amounts to saying, as only a supremacist of one sort or another can, "I know your reality better than you know it yourself." And so we must learn to listen, and to assume that folks of color are indeed the best exponents and chroniclers of their own experiences—far from perfect, but considerably more capable in this regard than we who have not suffered centuries of enslavement, domination, indignity, and alienation by another race.

So we must hear—and not just hear but really *feel* the words of black folks, like the young black student who told UCLA professor Jerome Rabow of her jarring experience with racism, not fifty years ago, but in the present-day.

I can remember as a child having a good friend . . . who I did everything with. We were the best of friends. [The friend] was white and I was black but that was never an issue. One day we were in her backyard playing in the snow. We were having a great time. I remember starting a snowball fight. Well, we were getting wet and cold from the snow and were ready to stop. I threw my last snowball and it hit [my friend] in the face. [She] became mad. All of a sudden she shouted, "Nigger" into my face. She kept repeating it. Soon her little brother and sister joined in. I started to cry. "Why were they saying this to me?" I felt so scared and helpless. I ran all the way home. That day I knew I was different.[112]

We have to hear—and not only hear but really *feel* the words of those like 22-year-old Calvin, who explained to author and anthropologist Annie Barnes his experience with racial profiling and oppression.

I went shopping at what used to be one of my favorite stores. I set my bags on the floor to free my hands to sort through clothes in my size. Before I could get halfway through a stack of polo shirts, two white guys came out of nowhere and jacked me up while the third guy dumped my things on the floor. White people were looking at me as if to say, "It figures. A black man is stealing." I've never been so humiliated in my life. They went through all my things but couldn't find any stolen items. Then they explained why everything happened so fast and why I had been handcuffed. The reason they gave for placing handcuffs on me was for their safety. That is, they said, "Because of past experiences, we wanted to guarantee our safety."[113]

We have to hear—and not only hear but really *feel* the words of a 21-year-old black woman from New York, who recounted a similar tale to Barnes.

Returning from an overnight trip to New York, I arrived at Langston International Airport in Virginia with only an overnight bag. I went outside the airport to look for my ride to Norfolk State University. While walking down a pathway to the parking lot, something told me to turn around. I did. I saw two white men. Jokingly, I said to myself, "They're probably following me."

Much to my dismay, soon after I turned around, they manhandled, took me into the bushes, and searched my bag. I asked them, "What are you looking for?" They said, "Drugs." I was shocked. . . . They asked, "Where did you get the schoolbooks in your bag? How long did you stay in New York? Did you have business there? Why are you in Virginia?" Subsequently, they requested my identification.

When they didn't find drugs and determined my identity, they told me to close my bags and left without an apology. Afterward, I spoke with a man, the black gardener who worked there, who had watched the search. He told me that only blacks were searched.[114]

Or the testimony, also given to Barnes, by Truitt, a 25-year-old black male, which further corroborates the ubiquity of anti-black suspicion and harassment in the nation.

> It was February 1993, and I was 23 years old. I was traveling by car from New Jersey to North Carolina. About 30 minutes into the trip, a white police officer pulled me over and said that I was driving 90 miles an hour; however, I had only been doing 60. The officer rudely made me get out of the car and ordered me to lie face down on the side of the highway. He called for backup and then began searching my car for drugs. While I was lying on the ground, the officer shouted out to me, "Nigger. I know you got drugs. Where are they?" I said, "There are no drugs." Then he answered back by saying, "Your black ass is going to jail today." Not finding drugs, he only wrote a speeding ticket and let me go. After driving away, I felt rage because it seems as if blacks can't get true justice in America.[115]

We must also learn to hear and really *feel* the pain and horror described by black survivors of the post-Katrina flooding in New Orleans, whose tales of mistreatment rival anything most have ever heard, or could have imagined hearing. To wit, the words of Patricia Thompson, a longtime New Orleans resident and flood survivor:

[D]uring the time we were across the street from the Convention Center, these cops—I don't know if they were police but they were all in black, they had these guns, and they were banded real close together—they came up the street, and they were screaming all kinds of obscenities, and all kinds of racial slurs. And they were pointing guns at folk and demanding you to lay down.

At this particular time, I had really gotten tired of using the restroom on the sidewalk, and so I'm trying to get across the street into the Convention Center to use the restroom. At this point, these cops, whoever they were, they came up the street, they got these guns with the lights on them, you know, they pointing them at people saying, "Sit your so-and-so so-and-so down before I blow your so-and-so head off, you black so-and-so."

I mean, God. At that point, it really felt like I was in the Twilight Zone. They're treating us like criminals. But everybody had to adhere to what they said, so once they passed me, I pretty much stayed low, in just about a crawling position, trying to get across to the other street to get into the Convention Center to use the restroom.

What I seen when I came out I will remember for the rest of my life. . . . At this time, I'm crouched trying to get back into the parking lot. . . . Everybody is sitting on the ground with their hands in the air. The cops are stationed in different spots, with their guns aimed on people. I look at my 5-year-old granddaughter, Baili McPherson, and the light from one of the guns was actually on her forehead.

My oldest daughter, Gayness, she's like, you want to go ballistic when you see someone do something like this to your child but you can't do nothing because, guess what, you and your child both might get killed. Baili is sitting with her hands in the air. And she's just past afraid, she's terrified. And she's asking her mama, Gaynell, "Am I doing it right?" because even the babies know the police kill in New Orleans. So she's asking her mama, "Mama, am I doing it right, am I doing it right?"[116]

And we must also listen to the elders who have lived through a racist white America so horrific that it seems impossible to be part of recent American history—but it is our history— and it is part of the living memory of many Americans alive today. These are the words of Alice Walker, written during the Obama campaign:

When I was born in 1944 my parents lived on a middle Georgia plantation that was owned by a white distant relative, Miss May Montgomery. (During my childhood it was necessary to address all white girls as "Miss" when they reached the age of twelve.) She would never admit to this relationship, of course, except to mock it. Told by my parents that several of their children would not eat chicken skin she responded that of course they would not. No Montgomerys would.

My parents and older siblings did everything imaginable for Miss May. They planted and raised her cotton and corn, fed and killed and processed her cattle and hogs, painted her house, patched her roof, ran her dairy, and, among countless other duties and responsibilities my father was her chauffeur, taking her anywhere she wanted to go at any hour of the day or night. She lived in a large white house with green shutters and a green, luxuriant lawn: not quite as large as Tara of *Gone With the Wind* fame, but in the same style.

We lived in a shack without electricity or running water, under a rusty tin roof that let in wind and rain. Miss May went to school as a girl. The school my parents and their neighbors built for us was burned to the ground by local racists who wanted to keep ignorant their competitors in tenant farming. During the Depression, desperate to feed his hardworking family, my father asked for a raise from ten dollars a month to twelve. Miss May responded that she would not pay that amount to a white man and she certainly wouldn't pay it to a nigger. That before she'd pay a nigger that much money she'd milk the dairy cows herself.

When I look back, this is part of what I see. I see the school bus carrying white children, boys and girls, right past me, and my brothers, as we trudge on foot five miles to school. Later, I see my parents struggling to build a school out of discarded army barracks while white students, girls and boys, enjoy a building made of brick. We had no books; we inherited the cast off books that "Jane" and "Dick" had previously used in the all-white school that we were not, as black children, permitted to enter.

The year I turned fifty, one of my relatives told me she had started reading my books for children in the library in my home town. I had had no idea—so kept from black people it had been—that such a place existed. To this day knowing my presence was not wanted in the public library when I was a child I am highly uncomfortable in libraries and will rarely, unless I am there to help build, repair, refurbish or raise money to keep them open, enter their doors.

When I joined the freedom movement in Mississippi in my early twenties it was to come to the aid of sharecroppers, like my parents, who had been thrown off the land they'd always known, the plantations, because they attempted to exercise their "democratic" right to vote. I wish I could say white women treated me and other black people a lot better than the men did, but I cannot. It seemed to me then and it seems to me now that white women have copied, all too often, the behavior of their fathers and their brothers, and in the South, especially in Mississippi, and before that, when I worked to register voters in Georgia, the broken bottles thrown at my head were gender free.

I made my first white women friends in college; they were women who loved me and were loyal to our friendship, but I understood, as they did, that they were white women and that whiteness mattered. That, for instance, at Sarah Lawrence, where I was speedily inducted into the Board of Trustees practically as soon as I graduated, I made my way to the campus for meetings by train, subway and foot, while the other trustees, women and men, all white, made their way by limo. Because, in our country, with its painful history of unspeakable inequality, this is part of what whiteness means.[117]

In a healthy society such testimonies as these would surely enrage. And yet it seems painfully apparent at present that the kind of openness needed to truly take in material such as this remains a precious commodity, far more rare than required if we are to move forward on the road to justice.

We must enter into honest dialogue about our national condition, without blinders. This means realizing that black and brown folk come to conversations on race with unresolved and largely unrecognized anger and pain. Thus, when cross-racial dialogue begins between whites and blacks, for instance, the trajectory of the discussion resembles, oftentimes, a dialogue between partners in an abusive relationship in front of a counselor. One partner doesn't want to admit that they have done anything wrong, or they claim that perhaps they did, but they were provoked; or maybe they weren't provoked, but it was a long time ago; or perhaps it was just last week, but they'll never do it again. And just as the abusive partner claims that sometimes their partner is abusive too (the infamous, "we push each other's buttons" line)—and indeed, it's true that abused partners do sometimes fight back, by yelling, throwing things, or even hitting—so too whites who seek to shift any discussion about racism onto so-called "black racists," and who hope to steer the conversation towards a discussion of black and brown flaws, rather than owning their own issues and taking responsibility for their own history of abuse.

Where the analogy with domestic violence fails, at least one hopes, is that in the abusive relationship between partners, the best advice is almost always for the abused to leave at the first safe and available moment. But when it comes to race, unlike the dynamic between domestic partners, whites and blacks are pretty much stuck with one another, if not in the same home, certainly in the same society. We cannot walk away. We must not. We are stuck here and must learn to make the best of it, but that will require courage and honesty, especially from whites who have been quite practiced at bigotry, cowardice, and deception heretofore.

Part of the process involves acknowledging—really listening—to folks describe their pain living with racism as a daily experience of violence, poverty, exclusion and denial. In other words, no more "Yes, racism has been horrible, *but . . .*" nonsense. No more semi-exculpatory clauses that have the effect, intended or not, of minimizing the gravity of the crime. No more "that was a long time ago," no more changing the subject to something else, and no more claims of competing victimization, as in, "Well, a black woman at the grocery shot me a nasty look yesterday," or "Some black kid called me a name when I was 11, so I know what it's like to face racism too."

Whites must be willing to hear (and grapple with) the oft-unspoken but real and disturbing history of their nation when it comes to race. Among the things we must learn to hear, and educate our children about formally through schools, houses of worship, and community groups, is the assessment of our nation's history offered up by folks of color. Among the chief impediments to productive dialogue and action to eradicate racism, white folks' inability to conceive of our nation in any but the most patriotic and un-self-critical terms is among the greatest. And so any significant indictment of American institutions, practices or policies, almost inevitably and within a blazingly quick time frame, results in allegations that the person leveling the charge is unpatriotic, hates America, and is unworthy of being taken seriously. Such an attitude often involves the discounting of almost all people of color, for most all black and brown Americans have experienced race-based inequity and recognize the deep contradictions, fissures and flaws embedded in U.S history, and most speak out about changing those flaws. The legacy of racism and the ongoing experience of injustice has bred and continues to breed much anger. But much of white America cannot countenance the anger, and this too must change if we are to move forward.

Many whites have always wondered aloud as to whence black and brown anger comes, and for what reason. Many whites appear never to have understood it, let alone agreed with its legitimacy. Perhaps this is because it scares them because it challenges the illegitimate premises of white control.

In the face of ongoing institutional racism in the United States today, black and brown anger is directed against the ongoing sources of injustice specifically, and at the ubiquity of white denial generally, at the obliviousness exhibited by most white folks—and often the callousness displayed by the same—toward black and brown exclusion and pain. The anger is also directed at white folks' almost maniacal need to hold onto and to propagate a historical narrative about the United States that bears virtually no resemblance to reality: one that allows only for the occasional mistake or minor shortcoming—all of which have been or ultimately will be overcome of course, thanks to the determined will of patriots—but never for the suggestion that America was founded on the basis of, and that many of its citizens continue to benefit from, centuries of abominable and sadistic acts against others.

To this end, the indigenous persons of the Americas died of diseases to which, sadly, they simply lacked proper resistance; and the enslavement of Africans was our nation's "original sin," to which, thankfully, Abraham Lincoln put an end; and Manifest Destiny, though perhaps a bit headstrong, was ultimately for the greater good; and our foreign policy disasters in Latin America, Vietnam, or the Middle East have been the result of "bad intelligence" reports, "blunders," or bureaucratic incompetence. But never, never the predictable outcomes of imperialistic doctrine. While other nations are run by tyrants who have no regard for human life, ours is run—or so most white people have long believed—by well-intended souls, who sometimes get it wrong but always have noble goals in mind and are merely the product of their times.

That such a convenient, and manifestly absurd rendering of American history makes sense to so many whites and seems equally preposterous to most people of color, suggests all we need to know about the heinous legacy of white domination and the depth and breadth of the nation's racial divide. It is as if millions of Americans occupy one of two utterly irreconcilable poles of reality. Those at one of these poles find it plausible that tens of millions of dead Native Americans, perhaps a million dead Filipinos, another two million or so Southeast Asians, hundreds of thousands of dead Iraqis, and hundreds of thousands more in Nicaragua, El Salvador, Guatemala, Haiti, Chile, Indonesia—and any number of other places where the United States has invaded, overthrown governments, or helped train and fund dictators and death squads—are merely coincidental. Those at the other pole are of the opinion that enough "isolated incidents" such as these, after a few centuries, constitute a trend, and might actually speak to the deeply racist and imperial national character, or at least those of its elites. Imagine.

So too, consider the deep divisions between blacks and whites in terms of how many in both groups view the basic trustworthiness of their government and leaders. And so, when the Reverend Jeremiah Wright suggested that the United States government may have deliberately created the disease complex known as HIV so as to target certain populations, much of white America lashed out (and took aim at Obama for his personal closeness to Wright), and not because they had examined the evidence for and against this admittedly controversial proposition, but rather, as a matter of patriotic principle. Many white Americans simply refuse to believe that U.S. leaders are capable of such a thing. This in spite of the abominable history of U.S. slavery, government involvement in medical experimentation, and acts of aggression against its own citizens: a history about which people of color, especially folks like Reverend Wright, are acutely aware, but about which many whites know nothing. For black folks, the idea that the U.S. government might be seeking to deliberately harm them is not the stuff of paranoid fantasy, or science fiction. It is the cognitive legacy of a very real history, in which U.S. policies, written and carried out by whites, brutalized black and brown peoples.

But most—and certainly most whites—have heard nothing of this history. They have never heard of the widespread medical and scientific experimentation carried out on black bodies dating back to the 1800s if not earlier by the white establishment. They know nothing of the fact that hundreds of slaves—including some owned by Thomas Jefferson—were used as guinea pigs for an experimental smallpox vaccine, even though the vaccine's efficacy was known to be questionable, and although the risk to those receiving it was substantial. Whites have never been taught of the experiments conducted on slaves, such as pouring boiling water down their spines to see if this might relieve them of typhoid pneumonia, or the gynecological experiments of celebrated physician J. Marion Sims, who subjected enslaved women to repeated and unnecessary surgeries to perfect his often painful techniques. Nor do they know about more recent, and yet similar atrocities, like the deliberate and massive dosing of mostly black patients with plutonium at an Oak Ridge, Tennessee, Army Hospital in 1945, intended to determine the risk of exposure to humans. Or research conducted by "scientists" and doctors at Tulane University and Charity Hospital in New Orleans, which involved grotesque and bizarre experiments on up to 300 black patients. As Law Professor Vernellia Randall notes:

> The experiments involved swallowing radioactive capsules and injections of radioactive mercury that resulted in blisters. The blisters were then intentionally cut open and subjected to up to 118-degree heat, causing diarrhea in the patients. While the stated purpose of the studies was to determine the effect of mercury on people with congestive heart failure, the 300 black patients did not have that disease.[118]

And most know nothing of the twenty-two black patients who in 1963 were unknowingly injected with live cancer cells as part of an experiment at a Brooklyn Hospital carried out by the United States Public Health Service and the American Cancer Society.[119]

Additionally, evidence of widespread medical experimentation and wrongdoing has been uncovered as part of the CIA's two-decade-long MK ULTRA program, exposed in 1975 during the famous Church Committee Senate hearings. Although the CIA chief at that time ordered all documents relating to MK ULTRA destroyed in 1973, so that the full extent of its operation would never be known, certain details have been officially acknowledged. According to former CIA agent John Stockwell—a thirteen-year veteran of the agency, former subcommittee member of the National Security Council, and former CIA station chief in Angola—the agency, as part of MK ULTRA, dragged a barge through San Francisco Bay and released a virus to measure its potential as a weapon, and launched a whooping cough epidemic in a Long Island suburb for the same purpose.[120] Additionally, as was revealed in the hearings, MK ULTRA included one project known as "Operation Teapot," which involved dosing pregnant women with high levels of radiation to study the effects on their developing fetuses, giving LSD to American soldiers to study the effects of panic, and irradiating the testicles of prison inmates in Oregon without their knowledge or prior consent.

Although many of the operations undertaken as part

of MK ULTRA were not racially targeted, several were. In the early 1950s, for instance, the CIA and Army Chemical Corps laboratory in Maryland bred millions of mosquitoes infected with yellow fever and whooping cough, and then released them in low-income black communities in Miami and in the Savannah, Georgia, area, to see how effective they might be as biological "weapons" against an enemy in wartime. The effect was a marked increase in mysterious illnesses and deaths in the communities used for the experiment. Although residents suspected they had been used as human guinea pigs, government secrecy kept the program cloaked by denial for more than twenty years.[121]

That the United States has, at various points, considered the development of weapons that would specifically target particular racial populations is a claim with strong evidentiary support, however much the public may not realize it. This very possibility was discussed in the pages of *Military Review*, a highly regarded defense journal, in 1970. And, as Harriet Washington documents in her recent volume, *Medical Apartheid*, a report by the Senate Select Committee on Health and Scientific Research suggests such a weapon may have been under consideration as early as the 1940s—specifically, it discusses research done by the University of California, supported by the U.S. military, to spread disease by way of fungal spores, especially to blacks and Asians. At a congressional hearing in the mid-1970s, one Pentagon official testified that the military had spread fungus in that fashion at a Naval shipyard in Virginia and at a loading dock in Pennsylvania—the latter chosen because the dockworkers were mostly black and "Negroes are more susceptible to the fungus than whites."

Or consider the charge by Wright to the effect that the U.S. government knowingly aided and abetted the distribution of addictive drugs in inner-city communities of color, a charge that first came to national prominence with Pulitzer Prize–winning journalist Gary Webb's 1996 reports in the *San Jose Mercury News*. While most of white America finds such claims preposterous, even libelous, many others, including a large number of folks of color, find the charge persuasive. And this difference in white and black perception has far less to do with black paranoia than white denial. That the U.S. government has been implicated in drug trafficking isn't really a secret to anyone who has merely paid attention to the openly acknowledged evidence that from time to time has trickled out publicly over the past several decades, in congressional hearings and elsewhere. Indeed, former CIA agents and operatives have themselves admitted to the role of American intelligence agencies in the fostering of the drug trade. Even the fairest, most modest reading of that involvement makes clear that these agencies, at the very least, knew that their operatives were trafficking drugs from Central America in the 1980s (and Southeast Asia in the 1960s and 1970s), and chose to turn a blind eye. Although non-enforcement of existing drug laws is not quite the same as deliberately planting drugs in American communities to destroy them—one is a sin of omission, the other, of commission—can we really say that they are any different? Do the parents of those whose lives have been destroyed by crack addiction really care whether or not the government gave Freeway Ricky Ross the dope, or merely turned its back while others did? Does the family who just buried their 5-year-old child, who was hit by a stray bullet fired during a drive-by shooting, really care about the subtle difference between intentional murder and mere reckless endangerment? Doubtful.

At the very least, the United States government has demonstrated by its inactions in the face of drug smuggling—smuggling they knew would create product distribution centers in inner-city communities rather than in the lily-white suburbs, and that would produce the violence and death that come as a result—that its priorities lay somewhere other than with the people over whom it governs. Overthrowing governments abroad, or supporting dictatorships, or furthering some other dubious foreign policy goal, has regularly and repeatedly taken precedence over protecting the American public. Or rather, the black and brown public, who always bear the brunt of the government's nonchalance, neglect, and worse.

In all of this I am being, of course, deliberately provocative, as was Jeremiah Wright when he inveighed against the militarism and racism that has marked so much of our nation's history. However unsettling such provocation may prove to be, let us remember that provocation is often what is needed in order to shake the complacency from the minds of the masses, not that anyone appreciates being shaken in such a manner.

Yet the white masses recoiled from Rev. Wright, both because of his tone and his content, much as they expressed outrage when Michelle Obama remarked that public responsiveness to her husband's campaign constituted the "first time" in her adult life that she had been truly "proud of her country." White folks never like angry black people, or even those perceived, as with Michelle Obama, to be angry, no matter the source of their anger, and especially if that anger be expressed in the course of administering a corrective to our self-imposed historical hagiography that passes for the national narrative. That whites were so offended, driven to distraction even, by the words of Jeremiah Wright, even as most black folks interviewed expressed agreement with the Reverend, tells us how deep runs the division between the races in our land. Could it be that they know something about this country we share, that we don't?

That most whites cannot conceive of an alternative version of the nation's history—one that is not laden with notions of American exceptionalism, but rather, one that takes note of the ways that the United States has behaved exactly as all empires behave, not worse, but often no better—suggests that what we are up against is no small force. Coming to grips with the notion that everything you know, or thought you knew, is wrong, and that everything you were taught is wrong as well, can be nothing if not unsettling. But unless and until we challenge, and stridently, the way in which white perspectivism blinds us to the national reality, the cycle of ignorance, denial, and complicity will continue.

As regards Obama this means realizing that the sunny and warm version of the American narrative that he pushes is not an accurate one either. He may say that the United States has nothing to apologize for with regard to our foreign policy—indeed he did say this during the campaign—but the people harmed by those policies would certainly disagree. Challenging white perspectivism will require us to come to grips with the distressing but true reality that Rev. Wright's version of American history was perhaps quite a bit more accurate than the version offered up by Obama in the process of disowning him. We can let Obama stick with whatever history he prefers, but we must insist on a different and more difficult national discussion for ourselves.

Please know that the need for this level of honesty is no mere ethical matter. It is a matter of survival. Being unaware of the way others see you is not simply unfortunate, but can often prove deadly. Ignorance, in this sense, is never blissful for long. And so the racist bubble of white denial and privilege, which allows those of us called white to avoid dealing with the perceptions and realities of others, can leave us woefully ill-prepared when danger calls. So on 9/11, it was whites and virtually only whites who responded to the national trauma of that day by wondering aloud, in sight of television cameras and the world, *Why do they hate us?* That most whites have no clue as to the answer speaks volumes, for there are few people of color who have the luxury of not knowing it. There are few people of color who have the luxury of remaining ignorant as to how they are viewed by others. Indeed, for blacks, and people of color more generally, survival has often depended upon having a keen sense of what others are thinking about them, and adjusting their lives accordingly. That whites have rarely if ever had to do this—to either think about how others might view them, or worry so much about how they were viewed as to actually change their behavior—may have served the privileged well up to this point, but in moments such as 9/11, that kind of ignorance can prove quite dysfunctional.

And so white America has long assumed that its rendering of the national history was a universally accepted truth, that the world has experienced the United States as it seems to have experienced itself: as a beneficent and gentle giant, spreading democracy and hamburgers for all the world. But this is *not* the way the United States is viewed elsewhere, and especially not in those nations that have felt the brunt of American interventionism, and where millions have paid for this interventionism with their lives. By not realizing this we put ourselves in danger. Not only are we inadequately prepared for something like 9/11, but more to the point, too many Americans respond to such an event with still more of the behavior that got us there in the first place. And so the privileged clamored for wars in Afghanistan and Iraq, even as people of color in the same nation evinced a great deal of skepticism that either would work as promised. And why? Once again, because to be privileged and virtually incapable of seeing yourself through the eyes of others, allowed most white Americans to assume that the U.S. military would be greeted as liberators. Meanwhile, most black and brown folks knew better, and opposed the attacks on Afghanistan and Iraq from the start. They know, as they must, that invaders rarely bring true freedom. They have been there, and done that, and bear the historical scars to prove it. And so here we sit, trying to find a way out of a quagmire of our own making, and one that stems directly from the hubris, the arrogance, the privilege of white America, which up to now has apparently been confident that it could go where it wants, do what it wants, and make the rules for the world. But that day is done. And to remain stuck in the fairy tale, in the fantasy, is to invite further loss of life and dignity.

On an even less global level, for white folks not to challenge racism is to perpetuate divisions that ultimately sacrifice the well-being of most everyone. When working-class whites ignore the commonality of economic need that they share with people of color, and instead act on the basis of racial bonding and exclusion—as millions did in this presidential election, unwilling to vote for the black candidate despite the fact that it was his policy proposals that would have reduced their taxes and benefited them most in terms of health care and education—they ultimately hurt themselves and only help to further entrench a politics of elite domination. Abolishing racism will require, as a prerequisite, redefining the current white conception of self-interest from racial terms to economic ones. It will require that we engage white Americans in an exploration of how, both historically and today, racial-interest thinking often stands in the way of true progress for all, regardless of color: how it has kept working people at each other's throats, fighting over the pieces of a pie that none of them, ultimately, own; how it has pitted white working class folks against immigrants of color and African Americans seeking greater opportunity for themselves and their families; how it has substituted the false promise of racial supremacy for something greater, something more lasting and meaningful—an economically supportive culturally diverse society.

Whites should discover and connect to the unheralded but significant historical tradition of antiracist white al-

lyship. To inspire this kind of rethinking we will have to connect the current generation of young people—especially those who were so inspired by Obama—to the long, if unheralded tradition of cross-racial alliance building, and for whites, to the tradition of white allyship. That our schools do a woefully inadequate job of teaching the contributions of people of color goes without saying; but so too do they ignore, typically, the contributions of those whites who stood shoulder to shoulder with the black and brown to forge a different path. Few have heard the names of Jeremiah Evarts, Angelina and Sara Grimke, Helen Hunt Jackson, John Fee, Virginia Foster Durr, Ellsberry Ambrose, George Henry Evans, Jonathan Blanchard, Laura Haviland, Robert Carter, Anne Braden, or Bob and Dorothy Zellner, among many others. Their brave resistance to white supremacy and racism—some in the days of slavery and Indian genocide, some in the Jim Crow era, and some well into the present era—suggests that although we might not have been encouraged to recognize it, whites do have a choice. If we know that, if we understand it and are encouraged to join people of color, and to exercise the option of resistance—if we, in other words, are inspired to live differently in this skin from the way most do—then we may yet forge the movement that so many of Obama's supporters thought they were already seeing in the midst of the presidential campaign. If we fail in this, however— if those young people inspired by Obama retreat into the laager of electoral politics and mainstream Democratic Party efforts—they will hook themselves to a train whose destination is always going to be toned-down, safe, easy, and unwilling to challenge the masses to think beyond the next election cycle.

Voting is a tactic: nothing more, and nothing less. It matters who wins—and frankly, those who doubt this, or who insisted there was no difference between Obama and McCain, have allowed their cynicism to grow to such proportions as to call into question their continued utility in the movement for social justice—but voting is no panacea. It is, as activist Chris Crass has noted, a method of harm reduction. Elections will never free the country from corporate-dominated politics, or two-party collusion with militarism and other national predations. But elections can buy us some breathing room, allowing for the space to organize.

Those who were involved in the Obama effort will now need direction. They will need some place to put all that energy, all that determination, and all that desire for a better world. It is hard not to be inspired by their passion, commitment and diligence. Here's hoping that we, as a nation, can be worthy of it in years to come.

Whites should speak up whenever and wherever we observe racism, overt or subtle, personal or institutional. Only with practice, with repetition, with sustained effort, can allyship for whites become second nature and a permanent feature of daily life in the United States. Indeed, white silence is the only privilege whites can voluntarily relinquish: the rest obtain as a matter of merely living as a member of the dominant group. That whites can opt for resistance will mean nothing, however, unless we actually choose to do so. This means in our schools and those of our children; at our workplaces; in our houses of worship, neighborhoods, community organizations, and families. It means critically assessing each and every policy, practice or procedure in place within the institutional settings where we operate, peeking under the hood of those structures to ferret out their inner-workings, and especially when those inner-workings are contributing to the maintenance of racial inequity and injustice.

Speaking out will not be easy: resisting injustice never is. And for white folks, so long practiced at maintaining our silence, it may well be among the more daunting tasks we have undertaken. But to not do it—to not challenge the racist remark, joke, policy or practice—is to collaborate with it, to give our assent, to undermine our personal and national pretensions to democracy. To remain silent, to fail in this endeavor is, in a strange way, to shirk our patriotic duty—to the extent we think such duties important--and to make our claims of national greatness out to be lies. It is to squander whatever progress we may take Barack Obama's election to herald, and to ensure that the change so many have hoped for will likely never materialize.

Perhaps the most important thing for all of us to remember is that which Martin Luther King Jr. tried to tell us in his last full book, *Where Do We Go From Here: Chaos or Community?*: namely, that "Change does not roll in on the wheels of inevitability, but comes through continuous struggle."

Endnotes

1. Jessie Daniels, "Ground Game in PA: Anti-Racist Organizing," *RacismReview.com*, November 5, 2008. Also, this author consulted with the Obama campaign in Ohio a few months before the election, specifically on how to address racism encountered by canvassers and phone bankers calling on behalf of Obama in working class communities. That the campaign was open to the suggestion that they couldn't merely "pivot" back to economics when racism was evident, but instead needed to confront it directly (albeit respectfully), suggests that the ability to turn the Obama experience for many volunteers into antiracist training may be stronger than many suspect.

2. I personally received several dozen e-mails during the 2008 campaign from Obama volunteers to the effect that they were often shocked by the extent of the racism they experienced during the campaign, and additionally heard stories to that extent from others across the nation who had worked for Obama, either as canvassers or phone solicitors.

3. "President Elect Obama," *Wall Street Journal*, November 5, 2008, http://online.wsj.com

4. Frank Rich, "In Defense of White Americans," *New York Times*, October 25, 2008.

5. Richard Cohen, "The Election That LBJ Won," *Washington Post*, November 4, 2008: A17.

6. *NBC News* transcript, "Decision 2008," November 4, 2008, 9:00 p.m., LexisNexis News, www6.lexisnexis.com.

7. Matt Bai, "Is Obama the End of Black Politics," *New York Times,* August 6, 2008.

8. Susan Page and William Risser," "Poll: Racial divide narrowing but persists," *USA Today,* July 23, 2008.

9. CNN/Essence Poll, July 23, 2008, CNN *Politics.com*.

10. New York Times/CBS Poll, *NYTimes.com*, July 15, 2008.

11. Paul Steinhauser, "In poll, African Americans say election a 'dream come true,'" *CNN Politics.com*, November 11, 2008.

12. The Gallup Organization, Gallup Poll Social Audit, Black-White Relations in the United States, 2001 Update (July 10, 2001), 7–9.

13. Joe R. Feagin, *Systemic Racism: A Theory of Oppression* (NY: Routledge, 2006), 166–167.

14. In the post-emancipation South, Black Codes restricted where African

Americans could live and work, in such a way as to virtually re-establish enslavement. In combination with vagrancy laws that essentially defined blacks without jobs or money as criminals and then leased them out to plantation owners and other commercial interests to "work off" their "crimes," these codes formed the backbone of late-nineteenth-century white supremacy. Additionally, massive violence against blacks swept the nation in the wake of emancipation. According to testimony in Congress, read into the equivalent of the Congressional Record at the time, literally tens of thousands of blacks were murdered in the first few years after emancipation: this on top of the several thousand whose deaths are recorded in official lynching records from the 1890s onward. For detailed analyses of post-emancipation oppression and violence see, Douglas A. Blackmon, *Slavery by Another Name: The Re-Enslavement of Black Americans from the Civil War to World War Two* (NY: Doubleday, 2008), and James Clarke, *The Lineaments of Wrath: Race, Violent Crime and American Culture* (Transaction Publishers, 2001).

15. Shawna Orzechowski and Peter Sepielli, "Net Worth and Asset Ownership of Households: 1998 and 2000." Current Population Reports, 70–88 (Washington, DC: United States Census Bureau, 2003), 2, 13, 14.

16. Thomas M. Shapiro, *The Hidden Cost of Being African American: How Wealth Perpetuates Inequality* (NY: Oxford University Press, 2004). With regard to white and black wealth disparities, gaps remain large, even when only comparing whites and blacks with similar incomes. So, for instance, among the lowest fifth of white and black households, in terms of income, white households average seven times the median net worth of similar black families. Among the top fifth of white and black households, in terms of income, whites still have median net worth three times higher than that of similar blacks.

17. Paul Street, *Barack Obama and the Future of American Politics* (Boulder, CO: Paradigm Publishers, 2008), 87.

18. United States Bureau of the Census, Statistical Abstracts of the United States: The National Data Book, 2007 (Washington, DC: Bureau of the Census, 2007), 399 (Table 613).

19. United States Bureau of the Census, Statistical Abstracts of the United States: The National Data Book, 2007 (Washington, DC: Bureau of the Census, 2007), 144 (Table 217).

20. United States Bureau of the Census, Statistical Abstracts of the United States: The National Data Book, 2007 (Washington DC: Bureau of the Census, 2007), 40 (Table 40).

21. Shapiro (2004), 7.

22. United States Bureau of the Census, Statistical Abstracts of the United

States: The National Data Book, 2007 (Washington, DC: Bureau of the Census, 2007), 40-41 (Table 40).

23. Michael Cinelli, "Survey Examines Asian Mobility," *Rice University News and Media Relations*, March 14, 1996.

24. Joshua Holland, "The American Dream, or a Nightmare for Black America?" *Alternet.org*, December 17, 2007.

25. Patrick L. Mason, "Race, Cognitive Ability, and Wage Inequality," *Challenge* (May-June, 1998).

26. Marianne Betrand and Sendhil Mullainathan, "Are Emily and Greg More Employable Than Lakisha and Jamal? A Field Experiment in Labor Market Discrimination" (June 20, 2004), http://post.economics.harvard.edu/faculty/mullainathan/papers/emilygreg.pdf.

27. Barack Obama, "A More Perfect Union," speech delivered at Constitution Center, Philadelphia, PA, March 18, 2008.

28. Devah Pager, "The Mark of a Criminal Record." *American Journal of Sociology*, 108: 5 (March, 2003), 937–75

29. Alfred Blumrosen and Ruth Blumrosen, The Reality of Intentional Job Discrimination in Metropolitan America–1999 (Intentional Employment Discrimination Project, Rutgers School of Law, 2002), http://law.newark.rutgers.edu/blumrosen-eeo.html

30. Barbara Bergmann, *In Defense of Affirmative Action* (New York: Basic Books, 1996), 44.

31. Gertrude Ezorsky, *Racism and Justice: The Case for Affirmative Action* (Ithaca, NY: Cornell University Press, 1991); Edward W. Jones Jr., "Black Managers: The Dream Deferred," in *Differences That Work: Organization Excellence Through Diversity*, ed. Mary C. Gentile (Cambridge, MA: Harvard Business School Press, January 1994), 65, 74–75.

32. William M. Hartnett, "Income gaps persist among races," *Palm Beach Post* (October 20, 2003): 2; Patrick L. Mason, "Race, Cognitive Ability, and Wage Inequality," *Challenge*. (May-June, 1998); Martin Carnoy, *Faded Dreams: The Politics and Economics of Race in America* (NY: Cambridge University Press, 1994), 47; Linda Faye Williams, *The Constraint of Race: Legacies of White Skin Privilege in America* (Penn State University Press, 2003), 359, Figure 7.1; U.S. Census Bureau, Statistical Abstracts of the United States, 2006; The National Data Book, Table 217, and calculations by the author.

33. "Major Study of Chinese Americans Debunks 'Model Minority' Myth," *ScienceDaily.com*, November 12, 2008.

34. Fred L. Pincus, *Reverse Discrimination: Dismantling the Myth* (Boulder, CO: Lynne Rienner Publishers, 2003), 18.

35. Feagin (2006), 196.

36. For extensive information about the history of housing discrimination and its consequences for the opportunity structure today, see, Melvin Oliver and Thomas Shapiro, *Black Wealth, White Wealth: A New Perspective on Racial Inequality* (NY: Routledge, 1995), and Douglas Massey and Nancy Denton, *American Apartheid: Segregation and the Making of the Underclass* (Cambridge, MA: Harvard University Press, 1998).

37. "Housing discrimination complaints at an all-time high," Press release, Department of Housing and Urban Development, April 3, 2007. http://www.hud.gov/news/release.cfm?content=pr07-032.cfm.

38. Douglas Massey and Nancy Denton, *American Apartheid: Segregation and the Making of the Underclass* (Cambridge: Harvard University 1993), 200.

39. Deborah L. McKoy and Jeffrey M. Vincent, "Housing and Education: The Inextricable Link," in *Segregation: The Rising Costs for America*, eds., James H. Carr and Nandinee K. Kutty (NY: Routledge, 2008), 128.

40. Joe R. Feagin and Karyn D. McKinney, *The Many Costs of Racism* (Lanham, MD: Rowman and Littlefield, 2003), 27.

41. Margery Austin Turner and Felicity Skidmore, *Mortgage Lending Discrimination: A Review of Existing Evidence* (Urban Institute Press, June 1, 1999).

42. John Wilke, "Race is a Factor in Some Loan Denials," *Wall Street Journal*, July 13, 1995.

43. "Special Report: Banking on Misery—Citigroup, Wall Street and the Fleecing of the South," 2003. *Facing South*. Issue 51, June 5.; Michael K. Brown, Martin Carnoy, Elliott Currie, Troy Duster, David B. Oppenheimer, Marjorie M. Schultz and David Wellman, *Whitewashing Race: The Myth of a Color-Blind Society* (University of California, 2003), 256, note 33.

44. Anthony Pennington-Cross, Anthony Yezer, and Joseph Nichols, "Credit Risk and Mortgage Lending: Who Uses Subprime and Why?" (Research Institute for Housing America, Working Paper 00-03, 2000).

45. James H. Carr and Nandinee K. Kutty, "The New Imperative for Equality," in *Segregation: The Rising Costs for America*, eds. James H. Carr and Nandinee K. Kutty (NY: Routledge, 2008), 22.

46. John Yinger, *Closed Doors, Opportunities Lost: The Continuing Costs of Housing Discrimination* (NY: Russell Sage Foundation, 1995), 66–75.

47. Judith R. Blau, *Race in the Schools: Perpetuating White Dominance?* (Boulder, CO: Lynne Rienner Press, 2003), 48

48. Gary Orfield et al., "Deepening Segregation in American Public Schools: A Special Report From the Harvard Project on School Desegregation," *Equity & Excellence in Education 30* (1997): 5–24.

49. Douglas Massey and Nancy Denton, *American Apartheid: Segregation and the Making of the Underclass* (Cambridge, MA: Harvard University, 1993), 153.

50. Kevin Carey, *The Funding Gap: Low Income and Minority Students Still Receive Fewer Dollars in Many States* (Washington, DC: The Education Trust, 2003).

51. McKoy and Vincent (2008), 131.

52. Carol Goodenow and Kathleen E. Grady, "The Relationship of School Belonging and Friends' Values to Academic Motivation Among Urban Adolescent Students," *Journal of Experimental Education 62* (1993): 60–71; Brenda Major and Toni Schmader, "Coping With Stigma Through Psychological Disengagement," in *Prejudice: The Target's Perspective*, ed. Janet K. Swim and Charles Stangor (New York: Academic Press, 198), 219–41; Kristin E. Voelkl, "Identification With School," *American Journal of Education* 105 (1997): 294–318; Daniel Solorzano, "Mobility Aspirations Among Racial Minorities, Controlling for SES," *Sociology and Social Research 75*, 4 (1991): 182–88; Philip J. Cook and Jens Ludwig, "Weighing the Burden of 'Acting White': Are There Race Differences in Attitudes Towards Education?" *Journal of Policy Analysis and Management 16*, 2 (Spring 1997): 256–78; Douglas Massey, Camille Charles, Garvey Lundy, and Mary Fischer, *The Source of the River: The Social Origins of Freshmen at America's Selective Colleges and Universities* (Princeton, N.J.: Princeton University Press, 2003), 9; Sarah Carr, "Coalition Says Study Rebuts Education Myths: Responses Demonstrate Commitment of Minority Students, Educators Say," *Milwaukee Journal Sentinel Online*, November 19, 2002.; Blau, Race in the Schools, 57–59.

53. Rebecca Gordon, *Education and Race* (Oakland, CA: Applied Research Center, 1998), 48–49; Claude S. Fischer et al., *Inequality by Design: Cracking the Bell Curve Myth* (Princeton, N.J.: Princeton University Press, 1996), 164–65; Leonard Steinhorn and Barbara Diggs-Brown, *By the Color of Our Skin: The Illusion of Integration and the Reality of Race* (NY: Dutton, 1999), 47.

54. Gary Orfield and Susan Eaton, *Dismantling Desegregation: The Quiet Reversal of Brown v Board of Education* (New York: New Press, 1996), 68.

55. Jeannie Oakes, *Keeping Track: How Schools Structure Inequality* (New Haven, CT: Yale University Press, 2005); Blau (2003), 54–55.

56. Saul Geiser, *Back to the Basics: In Defense of Achievement (and Achievement Tests) in College Admissions*. University of California, Berkeley, Center for Studies in Higher Education, Research and Occasional Paper Series, CHSF.12.08, July, 2008.

57. Russell J. Skiba et al., *The Color of Discipline: Sources of Racial and Gender*

Disproportionality in School Punishment (Indiana Education Policy Center, Policy Research Report SRS1, June 2000).

58. Centers for Disease Control and Prevention, *Youth Risk Behavior Surveillance—United States, 2005. Surveillance Summaries* (Washington, DC June 9, 2006), pp. 38, 40, 46, 54, 56, 62, 64, 66, 68, 70, 90; also, see the most recent data, from 2007, in, R. Dinkes, E. F. Cataldi, and W. Lin-Kelly, *Indicators of School Crime and Safety, 2007* (National Center for Education Statistics, Institute of Education Sciences, U.S. Department of Education, and Bureau of Justice Statistics, Office of Justice Programs, U.S. Department of Justice. Washington, DC, 2008).

59. Paige Harrison and Jennifer Karberg. *Prison and Jail Inmates at Midyear 2002* (U.S. Department of Justice, Bureau of Justice Statistics, Bulletin, April 2003), 1; *World Without Work: Causes and Consequences of Black Male Joblessness*. (Center for the Study of Social Policy and the Philadelphia Children's Network, 1994).

60. Human Rights Watch, "Race and Incarceration in the United States," Human Rights Watch Press Backgrounder, February 27, 2002.

61. B.W. Burston, D. Jones, and P. Robertson-Saunders, "Drug use and African-Americans: Myth versus reality," *Journal of Alcohol and Drug Education*, 40(2) (1995):19-39.

62. Substance Abuse and Mental Health Services Administration. *Summary of Findings from the 2000 National Household Survey on Drug Abuse*. Office of Applied Studies (Department of Health and Human Services, Rockville, MD., 2001), Table F.14, Substance Abuse and Mental Health Services Administration (SAMHSA), *Results from the 2002 National Survey on Drug Use and Health*, also, *Summary of Findings from the National Household Survey on Drug Abuse*. (Office of Applied Studies, Department of Health and Human Services, Rockville, MD, 2003)

63. Centers for Disease Control and Prevention, *Youth Risk Behavior Surveillance—United States, 2005. Surveillance Summaries* (Washington, DC, June 9, 2006)

64. Jim Sidanius, Shana Levin and Felicia Pratto, "Hierarchial Group Relations, Institutional Terror and the Dynamics of the Criminal Justice System," in *Confronting Racism: The Problem and the Response*, Eds. Jennifer Eberhardt and Susan T. Fiske (London: Sage Publications, 1998), 142; SAMHSA (2003): Table H.1., and calculations by the author.

65 . "Young White Offenders get lighter treatment," *The Tennesseean,* April 26, 2000: 8A.

66. Human Rights Watch, *Punishment and Prejudice: Racial Disparities in the War on Drugs* (Washington, DC May 2000).

67. Michael K. Brown, Martin Carnoy, Elliott Currie, Troy Duster, David B.

Oppenheimer, Marjorie M. Schultz and David Wellman, *Whitewashing Race: The Myth of a Color-Blind Society* (University of California, 2003), 144.

68. Matthew R. Durose, Erica L. Schmitt, and Patrick A. Langan, *Contacts Between Police and the Public: Findings from the 2002 National Survey.* (U.S. Department of Justice: Bureau of Justice Statistics, April 2005); and, Patrick A. Langan, Lawrence A. Greenfeld, Steven K. Smith, Matthew R. Durose, and David J. Levin. *Contacts Between Police and the Public: Findings From the 1999 National Survey* (United States Department of Justice: Bureau of Justice Statistics, February 2001): 2, 22.

69. David Harris, *Profiles in Injustice: Why Racial Profiling Can't Work* (NY: The New Press, 2002), 216–217.

70. "Study: LAPD Targets Blacks, Hispanics," *CBS News*, October 21, 2008, *cbsnews.com*.

71. National Abortion Federation, "Violence and Disruption Statistics: Incidents of Violence and Disruption Against Abortion Providers in the U.S. And Canada," http://www.prochoice.org/pubs_research/ publications/downloads/about_abortion/violence_statistics.pdf

72. American Civil Liberties Union, *Sanctioned Bias: Racial Profiling Since 9/11* NY: ACLU, February, 2004.

73. Brigid Schulte, "Life and death: an unequal proposition," *Miami Herald,* August 4, 1998; Joseph L. Graves Jr., The Race Myth: Why We Pretend Race Exists in America (NY: Dutton, 2004), 133; also, "Transcript: Race and Health: In Genes or Injustice?" The Gene Media Forum, November 14, 2001.

74. Graves (2004), 133.

75. See, for instance, Annie Barnes, *Say It Loud: Middle Class Blacks Talk About Racism and What to Do About It* (Cleveland, OH: Pilgrim Press, 2000).

76. Robin Smiles, "Race Matters in Health Care," *Black Issues in Higher Education* (May 23, 2002).

77. Shimon Weitzman et al., "Gender, Racial, and Geographic Differences in the Performance of Cardiac Diagnostic and Therapeutic Procedures for Hospitalized Acute Myocardial Infarction in Four States," *American Journal of Cardiology*, 79 (1997): 722–26.

78. Lisa M. Schwartz, Steven Woloshin, and H. Gilbert Welch, "Misunderstandings about the Effects of Race and Sex on Physicians' Referrals for Cardiac Catheterization," *New England Journal of Medicine 341* (1999): 279–83.

79. Dolores Acevedo-Garcia and Theresa L. Osypuk, "Impacts of Housing and Neighborhoods on Health: Pathways, Race and Ethnic Disparities,

and Policy Directions," in *Segregation: The Rising Costs for America*, eds. James H. Carr and Nandinee K. Kutty (NY: Routledge, 2008), 214.

80. Paul Street, *Barack Obama and the Future of American Politics* (Boulder, CO: Paradigm Publishers, 2008), 49.

81. That the Red Cross was blocked from entering the city by the federal and state Departments of Homeland Security (DHS) was made public within days of the flooding. According to the Red Cross website's "frequently asked questions" section on September 2, 2005, the DHS wanted them to remain outside the city so as to speed the evacuation of New Orleans.

82. This blatantly racist act has received virtually no media attention whatsoever, but has been confirmed by whites who were on the buses in question, in interviews with Lance Hill, Director of the Southern Institute for Education and Research at Tulane University in New Orleans, and also by time-stamped satellite photos, in the author's possession, which show the Orleans Parish school buses heading from a downtown bus barn to the pier in neighboring, mostly white St. Bernard Parish.

83. Bill Quigley, "Katrina, the Pain Index," *Counterpunch*, August 25, 2008, counterpunch.org.

84. Glen Ford and Peter Campbell, "Katrina: A Study—Black Consensus, White Dispute," *The Black Commentator*, 165 (January, 2006): 5.

85. Lizzy Ratner, "New Orleans Redraws Its Color Line," *The Nation*, September 15, 2008: 21–25.

86. Michael Eric Dyson, *Come Hell or High Water: Hurricane Katrina and the Color of Disaster* (NY: Basic Books, 2006), 21.

87. Gary Younge, "Murder and rape — fact or fiction?" *London Guardian*, September 6, 2005. Additional reports in *USA Today*, the *New York Times* and over the AP wire have followed Younge's original piece, and all of them have increasingly debunked reports of widespread violence and mayhem. For an analysis of the many falsehoods later disproved, see Jaime Omar Yassin, "Demonizing the Victims of Katrina," *EXTRA!* (Fairness and Accuracy in Reporting) 18:6, (December, 2005): 9–15.

88. A.C. Thompson, "Katrina's Hidden Race War," *The Nation*, January 5, 2009.)

89. "She's Got Lovely, Racist Eyes," *Rightwingwatch.org*, October 17, 2008.

90. Jonathan Martin, "It's Getting Ugly Out There," *Politico.com*, October 23, 2008.

91. Sam Stein, "Some Conservatives See race in Powell's Obama Endorsement," *HuffingtonPost.com*, October 19, 2008.

92. Peter Freier and John Atlas, "The GOP Scapegoats ACORN," *CBS News*, October 25, 2008, cbsnews.com/stories/2008/10/24/opinion/main4544472.shtml.

93. Dreier and Atlas (2008).

94. Though claims of voter fraud engineered by ACORN were ubiquitous in the month prior to the election, there was never any evidence to sustain this charge. What fraud had occurred was voter registration fraud, wherein persons employed by ACORN to register new voters essentially cheated their employer by filling out bogus registration cards rather than doing the work for which they were being paid. The only way such actions could have resulted in actual voter fraud, however, and thereby even theoretically have affected the outcome of the election, would be if the persons whose bogus names were entered on the registration cards showed up to vote on election day. That such bogus names included cartoon characters, professional athletes, and altogether made-up persons made such a likelihood remote to say the least. See, "ACORN Accusations," *FactCheck.org*, http://www.factcheck.org/elections-2008/acorn_accusations.html. October 18.

95. "Teacher's Aide Suspended Over 'Racist' Obama Remarks," http://www.thepittsburghchannel.com/cnn-news/17956560/detail.html.

96. Tommy Christopher, "School Children Chant 'Assassinate Obama,'" AOL News, November 12, 2008, http://news.aol.com/political-machine/2008/11/12/school-children-chant-assassinate-obama/.

97. Bill Bradley, "Why Is the National Press Ignoring Small Town Racism?" *Vanityfair.com*, November 12, 2008; Hannah Strange, "Obama Win Prompts Wave of Hate Crimes," Times Online/UK, November 17, 2008.

98. Jonathan Kaufman, "Whites Great Hope? Barack Obama and the Dream of a Color-Bind America," *Wall Street Journal*, November 10, 2007, A1.

99. Paul Street (2008), 42.

100. Tom W. Smith, "Ethnic Images," *GSS Technical Report No. 19* (Chicago: NORC, January 1991).

101. Lawrence Bobo, "Inequalities That Endure? Racial Ideology, American Politics, and the Peculiar Role of the Social Sciences," in Maria Krysan and Amanda Lewis, eds. *The Changing Terrain of Race and Ethnicity* (NY: Russell Sage Foundation, 2004), 19–20.

102. Eduardo Bonilla-Silva, *Racism Without Racists: Color-Blind Racism and the Persistence of Racial Inequality in the United States* (NY: Rowman and Littlefield, 2003), 17.

103. Joe Feagin, *Systemic Racism* (NY: Routledge, 2006), 26.

104. Brian Flood, "Study: race important in how whites judge quality of neighborhoods," *UIC News* (University of Illinois-Chicago), November 26, 2008, http://www.uic.edu/htbin/cgiwrap/bin/uicnews/articledetail.cgi?id=12599

105. Joe Feagin, "Naive Political Commentaries and White Racist Performances," blog post, *RacismReview.com,* April 9, 2008, http://www.racismreview.com/blog/2008/04/09/naive-political-commentaries-and-white-racist-action

106. Fournier and Thompson, 2008.

107. Michael Eric Dyson, *Is Bill Cosby Right?: Or has the Black Middle Class Lost its Mind?* (NY: Basic Books, 2006).

108. Sut Jhally and Justin Lewis, *Enlightened Racism: The Cosby Show, Audiences and the Myth of the American Dream* (Boulder, CO.: Westview Press, 1992), 17.

109. Jhally and Lewis (1992), 110, 8.

110. Tim Arango, "Before Obama There Was Bill Cosby," *New York Times,* November 7, 2008.

111. Claude Steele, "Stereotype Threat and African American Student Achievement," in *Young, Gifted and Black: Promoting High Achievement Among African American Students,* eds. Theresa Perry, Claude Steele, and Asa Hilliard III. (Boston: Beacon Press, 2004), 109–130.

112. Jerome Rabow, *Voices of Pain and Voices of Hope: Students Speak About Racism* (Dubuque, IA: 2002), 91–92.

113. Barnes (2000), 78.

114. Barnes (2000), 123.

115. Barnes (2000), 125-126.

116. Lola Vollen and Chris Ying, eds., *Voices From the Storm: The People of New Orleans on Hurricane Katrina and its Aftermath* (San Francisco, CA: McSweeney's Books, 2006), 128–129.

117. Excerpted from Alice Walker's widely posted essay "Lest We Forget: An open letter to my sisters who are brave," March 2008, *alicewalkersgarden.com.*

118. Vernellia Randall, *Dying While Black* (Dayton, OH: Seven Principles Press, 2006), 120-123.

119. Ibid.

120. John Marks, *In Search of the Manchurian Candidate* (New York Times Books, 1975).

121. Final Report of the Senate Select Committee to Study Governmental Operations with Respect to Intelligence Activities, book 1: 360, April 26, 1976: 522–523, cited in Harriet A. Washington, *Medical Apartheid: The Dark History of Medical Experimentation on Black Americans from Colonial Times to the Present* (NY: Harlem Moon, Broadway Books, 2006), 360–361.

ABOUT THE AUTHOR

Wise is the 2008 Oliver L. Brown Distinguished Visiting Scholar for Diversity Issues at Washburn University in Topeka, Kansas, an honor named for the lead plaintiff in the landmark *Brown v. Board of Education* decision. He is among the most prominent antiracist voices in the United States, having spoken to over half a million people in forty-eight states about racism and white privilege over the past two decades. He has trained educators, physicians, corporations, community groups, and others on methods for dismantling racism in their institutions, and his writings are taught in college classrooms across the nation. He is the author of three previous books: *White Like Me: Reflections on Race from a Privileged Son*; *Affirmative Action: Racial Preference in Black and White*; and *Speaking Treason Fluently: Anti-Racist Reflections from an Angry White Male*.